# Mastery of Excellent Teaching

Harminder Gill

Copyright © 2019 by HARMINDER GILL

Control Number ISBN:
Softcover: **978-1-77419-014-2**

All rights reserved. No part of this book may be reproduced or transmitted in any form or by any means, electronic or mechanical, including photocopying, recording, or by any information storage and retrieval system, without permission in writing from the copyright owner.

Print information available on the last page.

Rev. date: **12/02/2019**

To order additional copies of this book, contact:

**Maple Leaf Publishing Inc.**
3rd Floor 4915 54 Street Red Deer, Alberta T4N 2G7, Canada
1-(403)-356-0255

Cover creation : **Marissa Flordelis**
Layout : **Marissa Flordelis**

# **Acknowledgments**

I wish to thank Maple Leaf Publishing Inc. for the time and dedication to make this book possible. Thank you to specific past professors and teachers for making me the best possible student I can be. Special thanks to my past students and clients for the success they have achieved and will continue to achieve in the future. Seven – hundred (700) positive comments have been included in Mastery of Excellent Teaching.

# **Table of Contents**

Chapter 1: Brief History .................................................. 1-13

Chapter 2: The Educator ............................................. 14-30

Chapter 3: The Classroom ...................................... 31-44

Chapter 4: Instruction ............................................... 45-56

Chapter 5: Techniques Part 1 .................................. 57-65

Chapter 6: Techniques Part 2 ................................. 66-80

Chapter 7: Techniques Part 3 ................................. 81-92

Chapter 8: Effective Presentations ........................ 93-111

Chapter 9: Futuristic Teaching ............................. 112-122

Chapter 10: Evaluations ............................................. 123

# Chapter 1

# Brief History

One educator cannot receive all of the credit for success in the teaching profession. I like to present the development of education in the teaching profession that has lead to the success of successful educators like myself. Only then can we continue the development of excellent teaching across all schools for all countries? The goal of Mastery of Excellent Teaching is to help more educators improve their ability to teach in front of many students. Constantly unlocking information to maximize learning, how to use new tools, locate resources, and look forward to bright futures create excellent teaching.

It started about 700,000 years ago during the Paleolithic age, handmade tools such as bone, wood, and stone were used for hunting and gathering. Ancient calendars, maps, and primitive paintings came about during The Paleolithic Age. About 7,000 to 6,000 years ago, The Neolithic Age, the Neolithic people developed crafts such as brick making, pottery, spinning, weaving, basket making, and building boats and houses. About 5,000 years ago during the Bronze Age, ink was developed in Egypt. About 4,000 years ago, metal swords and armor were invented in the Middle East and Greece.

About 2,800 years ago, the abacus was invented in China, and about 2,000 years ago, paper was invented in China. Even during the early days, cuneiform mathematics textbooks which can be dated back to 2000 BC suggest that there were some forms of schools that existed in Sumer which is now Iraq. There is also evidence that suggests there were formal schools that existed in China during the Hsia and Shang dynasties.

Socrates was considered one of the great philosophers in the Western World. No records of Socrates have found, but his students Xenophon and Plato wrote probably most of his ideas. The Socratic Method involves the teacher asking a series of questions that leads the student to a conclusion. The method is effective by allowing a student to memorize knowledge, apply, and formulate that knowledge into refined answers.

During the Age of Pericles, there was a thirst of knowledge in Greece until there became formal education. Their own versions of formal education were created. Sparta is a Greek city-state that used education to help children to become effective in the military. They centered their ideas by developing courage, patriotism, obedience, and physical strength. Athens was another Greek city-state that came up with an education program that stressed intellectual and aesthetic goals. Male children attended schools that taught grammar, reading, writing, math and other subjects that are even taught today.

Plato was a student of Socrates and built upon his ideas. He divided three classes of people in society as the artisans, soldiers, and the philosophers, which should all be educated in their roles. Our school system even to this day has been influenced by Plato's ideas towards education and the breakdown of classes that people are a part of in society.

Aristotle was also a philosopher and was a student of Plato and Alexander the Great. He felt the importance and purpose of life is to serve and improve humankind. The quality of a society has a direct correlation to the quality of the education system. He felt it was important to make education a top priority. He was different from Socrates and Plato in which he took a scientific and practical approach to the education system. Those of us to this day who like to get a hands-on approach instead of thinking of great ideas have Aristotle to thank.

Greeks influenced the Roman education system. They helped a system of schools develop. Some of the young children after taking the time to read and write attended a graminaceous school to study Latin, literature, dialectics, and other subjects. The Latin grammar schools were similar to twentieth-century secondary schools. Quintilian was an influential Roman educator who wrote and recommended educational practices during that period.

The dark ages were a period where a little amount of records have been found. There was political and religious oppression during this time. The lack of people to learn more regressed in Europe. Formal education was not an option for everyone. Only certain people in the church or the wealthy had access to it. Charlemagne was a talented educator who selected Alcuin as a chief educational advisor who became famous during this time. Charlemagne also satin the Palace School with children furthering even his own education.

The church did not encourage common people in society to study the bible by themselves. They felt educated priests in the Roman Catholic Church should teach it. There was corruption during this period with priests because they felt so powerful. Thomas Aquinas changed the church's views on learning. He wrote the Summa Theological and formalized Scholasticism. He helped lead the creation of brand new learning institutions like the medieval universities.

Then the Renaissance age came. It represented the protest of individuals against the authority the church exerted over social and intellectual life. The Renaissance began in Italy when common people reacquired a spirit of free inquiry that was prevalent in Ancient Greek. The Renaissance spread through Europe resulting in learning called humanism.

In 1450, a German goldsmith Johannes Gutenberg took the time to perfect a movable-type printing press as well as a method to cast large numbers of letter type pieces. This type of device can be assembled anew for each page. It made printing to be faster and more affordable to the public. His invention made it possible for the first mass media leading to distributions to all types of reading materials. The public learned to read and become educated.

The Protestant Reformation began in 1517. Martin Luther published a thesis about his disagreements with the Roman Catholic Church. He wanted even the common people to read the bible. The Roman Catholic Church was afraid to let common people think on their own, but Martin Luther argued for the importance of education for all human beings. He wanted people to read and interpret the bible for themselves.

John Locke views' concerning the mind, and how common people learn have also influenced the American education system. He expressed his beliefs the human mind is a blank state and knowledge that is derived through experience. Harvard was the first colonial college to prepare ministers. Other schools formed such as Yale, Princeton, William and Mary, Brown, Dartmouth, King's College, Queen's College, and the College of Philadelphia were formed.

The Massachusetts Bay School Law made sure parents assured children know the principles of religion and the capital laws of the commonwealth. The Old Deluder Satan Act had every town of at least fifty families hire a schoolmaster who could teach children to read and write. All towns of at least a hundred families should have a Latin grammar schoolmaster to help them be accepted to Harvard College.

The New England Primer was the first reading for the American Colonies. It was a successful textbook published in the eighteenth century that also became the foundation of most of the schooling before 1790. Later on in 1693, John Locke published his views on educating upper-class males to be moral, rational thinking, and reflective.

In 1700, wooden paddles had printed lessons on it during this colonial era. The paper contained the alphabet and religious verses, which young children would copy to help them be able to write. If the children did not memorize their verses, the Hornbook doubled as a paddle. During the 1700, Benjamin Franklin came up with the American Philosophical Society, which brought ideas to the European Enlightenment. He wanted there to be more trained skilled workers so he came up with the idea of a secondary school in Pennsylvania in 1751. The educational institution was first called the English Academy offering many different courses. The academy changed its name to the University of Pennsylvania.

In 1762, Jean-Jacques Rousseau described his views on education and the importance of early childhood education. In 1779, Thomas Jefferson came up with the two-track educational system for the laboring and the learned. Towards the late, Seventeen-hundred's (1700), which is known as The Industrial Age, Noah Webster wrote a Grammatical Institute of the English Language.

It consisted of three volumes: a spelling book, a grammar book, and a reader. The spelling book was later renamed the American Spelling Book and was often called the Blue-Backed Speller.

Remarkably, in 1801, James Pillans invented the blackboard. In 1820, the school slate was a learning tool, which is similar to what the modern tablets and iPad are based on. Thanks to Martin Luther in the Fifteen-hundred's (1500), who advocated compulsory schooling, the idea spread to other countries reaching the American State of Massachusetts in 1852 and was extended to other states until the year 1917, Mississippi was the last state to follow this compulsory attendance law.

In 1854, the Boston Public Library opened to members of the public. It was considered the first major tax-supported free library in the USA. As years progressed, Christopher Sholes invented the modern typewriter. It was known as the Sholes Glidden. In 1870, the magic lantern was thought of as the precursor to a slide projector. The device was able to project images printed on glass plates, and they were shown in darkened rooms to students.

In 1876, Melvil Dewey came up with the Dewey Decimal System. It is still a widely used library organizational and classification system. In 1884, Lewis Waterman patented the first practical fountain pen. Writing essays became easier. In 1891, Leland Stanford founded Standard University in memory of his son.

Greatness in the education system continued to pursue even further. High School curriculums were formed by the National Education Association to establish a secondary school curriculum. During the Atomic Age in 1900, pencils and paper were mass-produced and became readily available and replaced the school slate. The shift in writing tools was a great achievement. The Association of American Universities was founded, to bring educational curriculum to a higher level just like the European nations.

In 1901, Joliet Junior College in the city of Joilet and in the state Illinois opened which became the first public community college in the USA. In 1905, The Carnegie Foundation for the Advancement of Teaching was founded. The Foundation also encouraged the adoption of a standard system for seat time to high school credits. It was referred to as the Carnegie Unit. In 1909, Ella Flaff Young became the superintendent of the Chicago Public Schools. She was the first female superintendent in the school system and was even elected to be the president of the National Educational Association.

In 1916, John Dewey advanced the ideas of progressing the education movement making it an agent for democracy. In 1917, Robert Yerkes who was in the army became Chairman of the Committee on Psychological Examination of Recruits. Louis Terman was on the committee and had the task coming up with a group intelligence test. The team of psychologists designed the Army Alpha and Beta tests. The idea of having standardized tests laid the groundwork for standardized tests we take today.

In 1917, the first radio education program was developed. WHA started broadcasting musical educational programs on the radio. This was the basis for many of the teaching technologies we use today. In 1919, all of the states had funds to transport children to school. This was also the time for the progressive education association for reforming American education. In 1926, the Scholastic Aptitude Test or known as the SAT was administered. It was based on the Army Alpha Test. The test as we know today assesses a student's readiness for universities.

In 1930, the overhead projector was used in school settings and many other organizations. It was initially used for training for the U.S. military in World War II. In 1938, the ballpoint became popular in the classroom and life in general. In 1939, Professor Frank W. Cyr at Columbia University Teachers College organized a conference to have adopted standards for the nation's school buses. David Wechsler developed the Wechsler Adult Intelligence Scale. It came up with the concept of deviation IQ. It calculates IQ scores showing how far subject scores deviate from the average score of the same age. The tests are still used today to help identify students who need special education.

During late 1940 until 1956, the computer age became about with the Electronic Numerical Integrator and Computer or known as the ENIAC. It was a first vacuum-tube computer, and Presper Eckert and John Mauchly first built it for the US military. This had to be one of the greatest inventions that really have had such a positive impact on our schools and everyday life.

During the middle of 1950, The Electronic Age continued to revolutionize society's standard of living. In 1950, William Oughtred and other people came up with the idea of using the slide rule based on logarithms by John Napier. Before the pocket calculator was used, the slide rule was used for the sciences and the engineering fields. It was not until 1974, the electronic scientific calculator made it obsolete.

During early 1960, there were many channels for television, which included educational programming. The Skinner Teaching Machine was invented, which allowed students to proceed at their own pace learning the material. This is based on the computerized learning systems that work today. Computers used in public schools were first used to teach elementary student binary arithmetic in New York. Everett Franklin administered the first ACT test in November 1959.

The photocopier became more standard in its use in the school system. It was introduced by Xerox and slowly replaced copies made by Fairfax, Photostat, carbon paper, mimeograph machines, and other machines that duplicate paper. Language laboratories and headphones also came common in school settings. It was used as an aid to teach languages through drills and repetitions. These language laboratories laid the foundation for many computer languages learning we use today. Sesame Street was used to create a children television show to help children prepare for school.

ARPANET that stands for Advanced Research Projects Agency Network was the precursor of the internet, and the U.S. Defense Department created it. Herbert R. Kohl's book "The Open Classroom" promotes open education. It emphasizes student-centered classrooms and learning being taken place. Handheld calculators paved their way into classroom settings. Jean Piaget's book "The Science of Education" was published. The learning cycle model helped people learn about the discovery-based approaches used mainly in the sciences.

Apple computers and IBM computers became common in classroom settings as well. More software programs became common such as Microsoft Windows and Microsoft PowerPoint. People started having their own personal computers at home as well. Multimedia features were also added to computer programs. The Apple iPad and much smaller more powerful versions of the computer were brought in the market. Homeschooling also became common for those students who did not attend a public school.

Another great achievement was the development of whiteboards that replaced blackboards due to some students being allergic to chalk dust and the ease at which marker boards can be cleaned. The smartboard, which is an interactive whiteboard that came and developed by Smart Technologies. Even CompuHigh was founded and was probably the first online high school. Google co-founders Larry Page and Sergey Brin set up their workplace in the garage at Menlo Park, California. Most schools now use google software to run some technology.

The Higher Education Act was amended and required institutions to produce report cards about the education performance for teachers. The flipped classroom is a teaching method that involves a student's instruction that takes place outside of the classroom through interactive digital experience where homework is being done in class with the teacher and other students helping. This is usually coupled with trends such as project-based learning.

On January 8, 2002, President George W. Bush signed into law The No Child Left Behind Act approved by Congress. It mandates high-stakes student testing, holds schools accountable for their ability to achieve at the desired level and gives penalties for schools that do not meet the goals of the No Child Left Behind Act. Many educational online classes have been developed for several people all over the world to take whether it is past subjects or subjects those who are interested in learning. The iClicker also came out to be a tool that allows educators to poll students in real-time.

During this twenty-first century, we now see great progress in teaching many students based on the development and inventions of the past. However, there still lacks that element based on how we teach students and the ability to teach well. The focus of the book is the educator. Both the format and style of the book is supposed to be user-friendly and provides techniques, strategies, and tools for effective quality of teaching. Educators have a powerful and longlasting influence on their students. They affect what they learn, how they learn, how much they learn, and how they view and interact with the world around them.

Educators need to promote positive results in the lives of their students if we are going to improve society. Desirable outcomes include high scores, positive attitudes, motivation, and interest to continue to learn. The book serves as a resource for those willing to demonstrate quality effective teaching.

Students who are taught by educators with better verbal ability learn more than those who are taught by educators with lower verbal ability. There is a positive relationship between educators who have the high verbal ability and student achievement. Fully prepared educators who have background knowledge of pedagogy have a better idea of recognizing individual needs and can customize instruction to increase student achievement. Better professional preparation can provide students with diverse opportunities to learn. Educators with coursework in education are better at classroom management, curriculum development, motivation, and teaching strategies.

As well as having content knowledge, they can anticipate potential difficulties and redirect the lesson to meet the needs of the students. There is also a positive relationship between student achievement and an experienced teacher taking the time for professional development opportunities such as conferences, workshops, or classes. Being able to apply and integrate both knowledge and skills is a key characteristic to being an effective educator.

# Chapter 2

# The Educator

Educators are professionals. Educators are managers. Educators are unique. Working with students is a skill that should be learned. Never put a student down in class in front of others. Work with parents to help their children succeed because you will not win without them. Effective educators also take the time to plan and organize. Make your expectations clear and consistent. Tell students what you expect of them and hold them to your expectations. Do not worry what your students think of you now. It is not as important as to what they think of you in the future. Do not be afraid to be less than being perfect. Do not be upset at something you cannot control.

Let us talk about the teacher as more than just a person does. The role of caring is important because it can be thought of as bringing out the best in students by affirmations and encouragement. Qualities such as trust, honesty, patience, and courage should always be there. Caring also includes listening, understanding, getting to know the students, being fair, being respectful, having enthusiasm for learning, and a positive attitude for the teaching profession. Let us talk about each of these fine qualities.

Effective teachers care about the students and demonstrate to their students that they are aware of it. We can define it as the act of bringing out the best in students by affirmations and encouragement. Again, I am talking about going beyond the qualities of patience, trust, honesty, and courage. Best teacher attributes show caring to include listening, gentleness, understanding, getting to know the students as individuals, and encouragement.

Effective teachers focus on sympathetic listening to show that they care about them in the classroom and their lives as well. There should be a two-way communication that shows trust, tact, honesty, humility, and care. They pay attention, understand what the students have to say, and are dedicated to helping students improve their lives and show their understanding through tenderness, patience, and gentleness.

Students value teachers who understand their concerns and the questions they bring. They want teachers who listen to their arguments and assist them in working out their problems. They want teachers who have mutual respect and who are willing to talk about their personal lives and experiences. Teachers start to become human through the eyes of students. Being available for students and their breadth of knowledge of the teacher's understanding makes the teacher a person demonstrating concern and empathy toward students. Effective and caring teachers know students both formally and informally. They do their best at every opportunity at schools and communities to keep the lines of communication open and honest.

They know their students individually based on learning style and needs and understand their personalities such as their likes, dislikes, and personal situations that affect behavior and performance in school.

Effective teachers care for the student first as a human being, and then as a student. They should respect each student as an individual. Caring teachers who take the time to get to know their students create relationships that enhance the learning process. Effective teachers consistently emphasize their interest in their students as an element of their success. Teachers who create a supportive and warm classroom setting tend to be more effective with all of their students. Caring teachers are initially aware of student cultures outside the school setting. They believe each student has a right to a caring and competent teacher. Teachers appropriately respect confidentiality issues when dealing with students. They also regard the ethics of care and learning as important when educating students to their full potential.

Effective teachers also establish rapport and credibility with students by modeling fairness and respect. Both respect and equity are prerequisites for effective teaching in front of students. Effective teachers deal with misbehavior at an individual level instead of holding the whole class responsible for the actions of a student or a small group of students. They carefully understand the facts before responding to a disciplinary situation, and then privately tell the students what they did wrong. They tell their students what they need to do right. Students expect their teachers to treat them equitably whether they behave or misbehave and avoid demonstrating favoritism.

Effective teachers continue demonstrating both respect and understanding along with fairness regarding cultural background and gender. Students expect their teachers should not allow ethnicity to affect the treatment or expectations of students. Students link respect with fairness to treat them as people. They perceive effective teachers as those who avoid being ridiculed and prevent situations where students lose respect in front of their peers. The professor should provide more consistent and better opportunities for students to have input in the classroom. Effective teachers offer students opportunities to participate and succeed.

It is given that both students and teachers spend a lot of their time during the day interacting in the academic environment. The ability to relate to students and make positive connections plays a significant role in cultivating a positive learning environment and promoting student achievement. Effective teachers use many strategies to interact with students.

The basis of these interactions goes beyond the classroom setting. Effective teachers show interest in students' lives outside the classroom setting. They attend special programs such as concerts and their students value sporting events in which students participate. Constructive social interactions between teachers and students contribute to both learning and achievement and increase student self-esteem by fostering feelings belonging to the classroom and the school setting.

Effective teachers are aware of their style of interacting with students, and they can provide a favorable learning environment for all students. Having social interactions with students, effective teachers can individually and successfully challenge each student to succeed. Effective teachers behave in a friendly manner while maintaining appropriate teacher-student role structure. They work with students as opposed to doing things against them. They also provide productive interactions giving students responsibility and respect, and they treat secondary students as being adults.

Effective teachers allow students to participate in decision-making, and they pay attention to what students are saying. Spending more time interacting and working directly with them shows effective teaching. Having a sense of fun and a willingness to participate adds excitement to the teaching profession. Add humor and be willing to share appropriate jokes also adds to effective teaching.

Be sure to promote enthusiasm and a desire for learning. The teacher's enthusiasm for teaching, learning, and for the subject matter has always been an important the element of effective teaching in supporting positive relationships with students and encouraging student achievement. Effective teachers can motivate most of their students by encouraging them to be responsible for learning, maintaining a classroom environment, setting high standards, and providing reinforcement and encouragement during specific tasks. This is how students see effective teachers as motivational leaders.

Effective teachers have positive effects on their students who are willing to work to their potential above and beyond. Less effective teachers can cause an interesting subject to become dull and boring. It is okay to let students sit quietly at the side, but they do not stop involving them. By continuously finding ways to motivate students to learn, a teacher contributes to a student's attitude towards interesting and fun activities.

Effective teachers can bring out the best in their students and understand students vary in different motivational levels. They know how to support intrinsically motivated students and continue to seek ways to provide extrinsically motivation to the students who need it. Motivating students makes students receptive to and excited about learning and making them important to the learning environment. Always provide positive attitudes and perceptions of learning, which allows the effective teacher to make the learner feel comfortable in the classroom setting.

Make sure you provide mastery learning techniques to provide the best possible outcome. They increase their interest in the subject, and a desire to continue to learn more about the subject. I just cannot stress how important it is to emphasize higher mental processes along with mastery learning strategies that make a learning environment exciting and helpful.

Keep these important points in mind when carrying out effective instruction. High levels of motivation of teachers relate to high levels of achievement for students. The teacher's enthusiasm for learning of the subject matter is a crucial factor in student motivation, which closely links student achievement. An effective teacher with higher degrees indicates enthusiasm for learning and maybe a source of motivation that translates into higher achievement among students. Enthusiasm for teaching gives overall effectiveness.

Your attitude towards the effective teaching becomes an important facet. Your dedication to students and to the job of teaching always needs to be there. There should be a dual commitment to student learning and to personalize learning. There needs to be a multitude of tactics of reaching out to students. Effective teachers see themselves as being responsible for the success of their students. They truly believe that all students can learn. They must believe in their students, their subject, and in themselves while continuing to know that students learn differently. Through different styles of instruction, effective teachers reach their students, and together they both enjoy their successes.

Effective teachers work collaboratively with other staff members. They share their ideas and assist other teachers with their difficulties. Collaborative environments make positive working relationships and help retain effective teachers. Effective teachers take the time to volunteer to lead work teams and be mentors to new teachers. They are looked upon as informal leaders, and they are not afraid to take risks to improve education for their students. Effective teachers are the individuals' administrators call on for opinions and help to effect the change.

Effective teachers invest in their own education. They model to their students that both education and learning can be valuable by taking classes and participating in professional development, conferences, and in-service trainings. They discuss the participation of these activities with students in a positive manner. Effective teachers learn and grow as they expect their students to continue to learn and grow. They serve as powerful examples of lifelong learners as they look for ways to develop in a professional manner.

Again effective teachers show positive attitudes about life and teaching. They spend extra hours preparing and reflecting upon their instruction on the well worth of student outcomes specifically when it comes to achievement. Participating in collaborative work environments results in positive attitudes for both students and teachers, and remembers effective teachers do not make excuses for the the outcome of student's performance. They hold students responsible while accepting responsibility for themselves.

Another factor of professionalism is reflective practice or the careful review of one's own teaching process. You should be able to continuously practice self-evaluation and self-critique as learning tools. Reflective teachers see themselves as students of constant learning. They become curious about themselves and about the art and the science of teaching. They always seek to improve lessons, think about how to reach their audience and seek new approaches in the classroom setting to meet the needs of their learners.

Effective teachers seek a greater understanding of their teaching through scholarly studies and professional readings. They monitor their teaching because they want to be better teachers and make a difference in the lives of their students. They are also not afraid of feedback, and they elicit information and construction criticism of others. The process requires open-mindedness, honesty, and time to change teaching behaviors.

Thoughtful questions guide effective teachers in reflecting on practice, which is crucial to lifelong learning and a professional necessity. Taking the time to reflect back translates to enhanced teacher efficacy. The teacher's sense of efficacy gives an impact on how instructional content is given to students. Efficacy does change for teachers as they encounter new experiences where they are likely to have more additional positive experiences. Their confidence in their ability to facilitate learning and understanding of material by students is observable to others. Effective teachers need to continue to be confident and be open to continue to improve their teaching practices. Effective teachers reflect on their work formally and informally. They have high student achievement rates on their work as an important part to continue improving their teaching. Maintaining high expectations for students is common for effective teachers who reflect back on their work.

Even though effective teachers can continue to maintain excellence based on their ability to teach, but they also need to interact well with a variety of people from all walks of life including students but also parents, coworkers, and bosses. Being skilled in dealing with people is not easy, but it can be done in the work environment and in all aspects of life. You heard the saying there are over all aspects of life. You heard the saying there are over thousands of things that go on in the teaching profession. It is not all teaching. Other issues take place in the teaching profession whether it is public or private school setting.

Conflict is inevitable in our daily lives. A hot conflict is where, one or more parties are highly emotional such as both parties speaking loudly, being physically aggressive, using abusive language, and appearing out of control. Cold conflict is where; one or more parties are suppressing their emotions, being physically withdrawn, staying silent, or appearing frozen. Both types of conflict are not constructive.

Conflicts that are warm at an optimal temperature are far more likely to be productive. Resolving conflict in the teaching profession is necessary if you are going to succeed in this profession. Time should be your ally. Do not rush and act out anything otherwise, you might say or do something you could regret later on.

Take time to focus on the problem and not people. Keep an open mind how to solve the problem. Having a neutral third party can also be of help where the mediator needs to have a firm grasp of the situation to make a conclusion. Treat others how you want to be treated. It might very well inspire your adversary to do the same thing. Remember when you are dealing with conflict, consider three main points handling it well and that is clarity, staying neutral, and having a considerate temper at solving the problem.

Dealing with difficult people rests upon how you are going to handle the problem constructively. Understand that most people act aggressively at work because they feel threatened. You may also want to ask yourself if you are being oversensitive or misinterpreting the situation. If someone else's behavior is inappropriate, then immediately deal with it and not wait.

Do not take the blame, and do not escalate the situation until you have tried to solve the problem with the help of your allies. Please do not continue to suffer. If the situation continues to go on and you can leave, then please do so for the best interest of yourself. Do not think you can change the person's behavior. Most people are angry because their needs are not met, but do establish a zero-tolerance policy.

When it comes to dealing with people in the work environment, establish a zero-tolerance policy and make sure you address inappropriate behavior in a consistent manner. Do not allow difficult people to set the tone for the classroom setting or even in the office, you work at. Dealing with difficult employees is also not easy so I encourage you as the educator to attend some seminars on resolving personal conflicts.

If there are problems whether it is in the classroom or office, deal with it immediately and do not wait for the last a moment or it might be too late. I encourage you, as the educator to be a good listener, work out a solution, and follow through on a plan of action but at the same time you has to understand how to perceive other personality traits.

The other party needs to understand, and if matters seem serious, it is acceptable to add some humor to lighten up the conversation.

Express confidence that the problem person will change and thank them for cooperating. Sometimes handling difficult conversations is carried out at the right time and right place. The objective is a win-win situation that will make both parties happy. It may also be a good idea to seek a trusted older person's advice. Only consult with a lawyer as a last resort since that is the time matters get real serious and ugly.

Many situations go on in the teaching profession, but do not take the problems in the work environment and bring them home. Leave the garbage back there and enjoy your personal life. If you have co-workers, bosses, or students who threaten violence then you need to monitor and document these situations before it gets out of hand. Sometimes, the best way to deal with a problem person is to just ignore them and let it go. Take the time to establish a system of complaints. Do your best not to take disputes personally. You are the authority in the teaching profession, and I hope you can set a positive example of such professional behavior.

I also encourage managers to communicate any problems up the chain of command. However, please do not become a parent for a difficult employee; it is not your job to do so. When working with groups of co-workers on a project or even having students work together on projects, make sure all team members are working together effectively. When team members do not pull in their weight to help the team, they are pulling down on the success of the team and should be let go.

In any profession including the teaching profession, be able to accept change and do not resist it. If you know of someone struggling, then do take the time to help or let your supervisor know about it. The success of any professional business including teaching depends on everyone rising to the challenges for the day. Provide more teaching and training opportunities for your students when it comes to time-management.

Use evaluations to help students be better students and keep an eye out for students of any inappropriate computer and internet usage. As for managers, stay away from the abusive ones out there. There is no need to work for an abusive manager if that manager is not helping you and making your life miserable. This is where all professionals need to take sensitivity training when it comes to dealing with people whether it is students, co-workers, bosses, and any person whom we have contact with.

When dealing with students, discourage the workaholics. The most successful people in life are the people who balance work and life. Then the next groups of people are the people who just work and study and have no social time. The last groups of people who are not successful are those who continue to have fun without working or studying. Workaholics do not always have the best for others since their personalities can become sour due to tiredness.

Nevertheless, that does not mean we should not celebrate successes. I want you to continue to congratulate and encourage those who succeed because it helps a person grow and continue to work hard. Speaking about successes, you will be more successful in your profession if you take the time to learn about your workplace rights. This is where I encourage you to seek help and get to know your Human Resource Manager.

There are backstabbers in the work environment. The best way to control the backstabbers is to extract the truth from them. They seldom survive head-on confrontations. Choose your friends as those colleagues who share your values. Avoid chronic interrupters by setting boundaries and do not let an aggressive colleague take charge of your meeting. I also discourage eavesdropping since it is a waste of time. If someone is having a bad temper, disarm the problem by taking the time to solve the problem. Being skilled at dealing with the public requires striking a balance of solving the problem where both sides become a win-win situation.

It is difficult to achieve respect and trust from the public. Once a person lies or makes up a story, it is hard to re-establish both trust and respect. Beware of false confidants whether it is your boss, co-workers, or even your friends in daily life. They are there to get loose information from you so they can pass it on to others.

I encourage you to keep your secrets to yourself. If you share your secrets with an unconfirmed confidant, you could be feeding information that can get you entangled with an arch-nemesis who could create problems for you. You do not want to empower an enemy and never assume someone is a confidant because more likely they are not.

Beware of those who think they are mind readers. The brain is still complex and we still do not know a lot about it. No one can read the mind and coming up with a false conclusion could lead you to be embarrassed and/or hurt an innocent person. Beware of the manipulator in the work environment or even dealing with students or people in our daily life. Some co-workers love playing the game of manipulation. The strings they attach to friendships are not visible until something goes wrong.

The best thing to do to handle manipulators is with evenhandedness. I do not recommend going along with them for being the nicest people in society. If you do not feel comfortable doing something, then do not do it. That will expose their real attitudes every time they are trying to get something from you. Having friendships with expensive price tags is not worth it and definitely, they are not your friends.

Beware of the minimizers in the teaching profession since they may not understand all of your problems. We cannot think that everyone is trained in therapy and will give the best comfortable advice we need or to cheer us up. Some people do the opposite and can make matters worse by making us feel worse. I encourage you to stay with those people. Nevertheless, at the same time, I ask that you continue to focus on the goodness in everything you do.

Dealing with bosses is also not easy but when you cannot get along with your boss, manage the situations to make the relationships work. Again, make sure the situation is a win-win situation, and if it still does not work out then the best strategy is to move on. Stay away from debatable topics and keep the conversations professional to the job at hand.

The last topic I want to discuss dealing with people is the topic of sexual harassment. Avoid office romance in the work environment. Keep the work environment professional and fair to all those around you. The media has portrayed men harassing women, but understand that women can also harass men and women can harass women and even men can harass men. Vengeful women are out there in society who lies to get innocent men into trouble. Some of them are oversensitive whereas some of them are not oversensitive. Either way, if they hate you for who knows what reason, they will cause trouble for you.

If you are sexually harassed in the teaching profession, take time to admit you have a problem. You need to let the person who is bothering you to stop his or her behavior and tell someone you trust about the problem. Get a copy of your employer's sexual harassment policy and take time to read it. I also encourage you to keep a diary of everything that happens which includes the names, dates, and the events that take place.

If the problem does not stop, then report the person to the proper authorities and cooperate with the investigation. If you are not satisfied, then it is best to look for an outside agency to help. Consulting with a lawyer should be the last resort if all else fails. Spending a lot of money and time to resolve the issues may or may not be with your time. You have to decide if you want to continue working in that same place or if it is time to move on.

Let us look at the other side of the sexual harassment issue when someone accuses you of sexual harassment. Take time to listen to the target's concern and take the situation seriously. Educate about the policies and procedures of sexual harassment through your Human Resources Manager. Encourage to let your fellow workers state what behavior is acceptable and not acceptable.

Avoid any behavior that is not acceptable. Find out what support and advice you need, get it, and evaluate the options.

Find a way to reach an amicable solution. The best the thing to do, as an educator is to get to know your expertise in your chosen profession and understand diverse groups of people in society.

# Chapter 3

# The Classroom

Effective teachers plan and prepare for the organization of the classroom with both care and precision to be used in a high-quality lesson. Components organizing the classroom include room arrangement, discipline, routines, and a plan to teach the students how the learning environment is organized. They envision what is needed to make the classroom or lecture hall to run smoothly. You want to create a positive climate and then work academic subjects into that atmosphere.

Effective teachers are educators who know how to support student learning through instructional techniques, have strong curriculum materials, and a positive rapport with the class. They need to create an overall environment conducive to learning. Having a supportive learning environment requires effective teacher practice skills in classroom organization and management. Consistency in behavior expectations and responses needs to be there. Effective teachers attend to these elements in a proactive way to establish a positive classroom climate toward learning for all individuals.

Being successful in classroom management involves more than carrying out the rules and disciplinary procedures. Effective teachers are those that are proactive about student behavior, which involves students in the process of maintaining rules and routines. They establish responses to any classroom issues that allow them to focus on maximum time and energy on instruction. When making the classroom experience engaging and carrying out fun learning activities, there is little time for those students to misbehave.

Effective teachers are prepared and keep their students actively involved in the teaching and the learning process. You always have to be ready for anything in the classroom setting. You may have heard the saying that, there are over a thousand things that take place in the classroom setting. It is not all about academic subjects.

Effective teachers are prepared for students almost every day including the first and last day of school. You want to create a productive classroom environment that includes planning such as coming up with functional floor plans with the teacher and student work areas, wall spaces, and furniture placed in the classroom setting. Self-preparation includes both physical and mental as important indicators for the organizational process. You need to be prepared for the difficulties of the workdays to create a setting that responds to different personalities. Always have a positive attitude to prepare students.

Again, you want to keep a good physical setting and establish the rules and procedures at the beginning of the school quarter or semester and continue to enforce these rules throughout the quarter or semester. Classroom managers effectively monitor students and are keen observers of student behaviors adept at addressing potential disruptions. Always be good at being aware of your surroundings since this always makes you effective at classroom management. Effective teachers should be aware of student behaviors when they tend to erupt and can quickly quell them.

Classroom management is influential in teaching effectiveness. Exploring student achievement, surveys of perception, and analyzing all the details in a classroom setting proves that effective classroom management is a key indicator of effective teaching. Elements of the best classroom management includes establishing routines and procedures that should limit disruption and continue to teach and maintain and monitor student activity.

Allow me to summarize again that having a consistent and proactive disciplinary procedures is important for effective classroom management. Effective teachers establish routines for their daily tasks and needs. They carry out smooth transitions and the continuity of momentum throughout the day. They also provide a balance between variety and challenge in student activities and have the ability to multitask.

Effective teachers should also have a strong awareness of all actions and activities taking place in the classroom setting. Best management skills include using the space and movements around the classroom to locate trouble spots and to encourage attention. The anticipation of problems that can arise by effective teachers is a skill that can limit disruption. They take care of small problems before they become big problems. Effective teachers can increase student engagement in learning and make good use of the time for every instructional opportunity.

Organizational skills are important when it comes to classroom management and when it comes to effective teaching. Effective teachers should be organized in terms of routines, behaviors, and the materials they use to better prepare for the class and set an example of the organization for students that allow organization for learning.

The organization has been shown to contribute to the best possible teaching outcomes. Some educators may argue that organization takes a lot of time away; but in reality, it allows smooth transitions between activities and increases time on academic, the fewer behavior problems take place in the classroom setting.

Effective teachers in well-organized classrooms prepare effective working environments by making good use of the materials for students. Both routines and procedures should be established so the classrooms can run automatically. Students need to know what to do each day and when they should be doing it. Effective teachers should provide differential instruction when it is needed.

Again, key elements of an organization include teachers multitasking and handling routine tasks promptly and efficiently. There should always be materials prepared and ready to use in advance for each lesson. It does not include extra materials in case there becomes an unexpected problem or sudden arrival of new students. Creating and maintaining practical procedures allow effective teachers to support students knowing what they should do, when, and with minimum repeating of directions. A strong communication skill is always a a necessary component in effective classroom management.

Even with strong communication skills comes the time where you are going to have to deal with managing and responding to student behavior. Effective teachers need to prevent negative behaviors. Most behavior problems occur because students do not know or do not follow routines and procedures. You need to be proactive when it comes to classroom management since this is the best and effective deterrent for discipline problems.

Take time to praise students, reinforce positive behaviors, and establish trust within the classroom setting will help you build respectful relationships between teachers and students. Disciplinary problems are not common in environments where both the teachers and students trust and respect each other. Again, the key to discipline problems is having strong management skills. Effective teachers manage and attend to students' needs.

It is awful when some teachers direct their attention and instruction more to some of the students and less to others. Providing more feedback that is positive to some people in the classroom setting and ignoring others will only create problems. This leads to students misbehaving in the classroom setting. Effective teachers should be able to recognize cues from students and decide if a predetermined the procedure should handle the behaviors. If there is no routine for there to be established, the teacher should quickly adapt to handle the situation with no disruption to other students in the classroom setting.

Effective teachers who reinforce clear expectations for student behavior will have more success controlling the classroom and fewer disciplinary problems than those who fail to do so. It is imperative that both rules and procedures should be established at the beginning of the school quarter, semester, or year and involving students in the process is effective approaches you can ensure students recognize their role in classroom settings.

Effective teachers continue to communicate and reinforce behavioral expectations. If the expectation is not met, the educator addresses the concern and allows the student the opportunity to identify the issue and provide examples of other choices the student could have made. The teacher assists students in understanding the logic behind the rules and the reasonable consequences for breaking the rules and the rewards for following them. Effective teachers link consequences to the behavior of the student. They handle discipline issues privately at the back.

There are times and situations that are not familiar to students where the teacher provides instructions on what to provide. Both parents and administrators should be involved in enforcing effective teachers well-prepared discipline plans. Effective teachers should believe that students have the capacity to learn self-discipline. Establishing behavior expectations should be consistent when carrying out responses for breaking the rules. This helps and achieves lower levels of off-task student behaviors in the classroom settings.

Effective teachers establish discipline carefully to support management in the learning environment. They should be able to handle the majority of it within the classroom setting without involving administrators. Reducing disciplinary problems in a classroom setting should significantly increase overall student achievement. It makes sense that the less disciplinary problems that take place, the more time there is for instruction, and if there is more time for instruction, then more students can learn in the classroom setting.

Effective teachers do their best to minimize discipline time and spend more time on instruction. The amount of time spending on disciplining students is inversely related to student achievement. Teachers need to interpret and respond to any inappropriate behaviors promptly, and they maintain clear rules and procedures and establish credibility with students through fairness and respect. Effective teachers reinforce the expectations for positive behavior. course, the line of communication needs to be open.

Organization and instruction are just as important compared to effective classroom management. Teaching can be a complex activity that should involve careful preparation and planning of objectives and activities on an hourly, daily, weekly, or even monthly basis. Long-term planning makes sure coverage of the curriculum needs to take place. Effective teachers demonstrate high expectations for students and select specific strategies for students in the learning process. Effective organization involves planning and preparing materials and involves the development of consciousness towards teaching and learning, and of course, the line of communication needs to be open.

Academic instruction needs to be central in its role as a teaching method. The focus on instruction should be implemented with planning, classroom behavior, and a safe learning environment. Effective teachers always see both consistency and organization in their classrooms because they allow focussing on classroom time on teaching and learning.

They always prioritize instruction and student learning as purposes of schooling to communicate an enthusiasm and dedication to teaching which students reflect on their behavior and practice. They also reinforce the focus on instruction by allocating time to the teaching and learning process and their expectations of the student learning process.

Time has always been a challenging constraint teacher's face when achieving curriculum goals and meeting the needs of all students while also managing administrative tasks which are necessary for the job. Effective teachers manage instruction through thoughtful and careful use of their time. Student achievement will be higher in classes where there is more instruction time.

Effective teachers prioritize instruction, which involves the use of time. They should remain with the students during the class period from start to finish and not waste time. Planning and pacing materials should be used to optimize time. Having a syllabus and providing it at the beginning of the quarter or semester helps the teacher plan and address the needs for the information. Sharing with students how the teacher organizes time serves as a model for students to assist their own planning, equips them with the tools of success for the real world, and instill good habits of efficiency.

Maximizing time allocation can also be carried out using stage areas. Doing one set of tasks at a time and carrying out the next set of tasks is essential for organization, which also leads to effective teaching. The effective classroom or lecture hall is a place for everything where everything is in its place. Establish a pattern so students will anticipate academic transitions, which reduce the loss of instructional time. Students should observe the routine and know what will occur.

Examples of effective time management can include giving students constructive use of their time during a class change by having them keep busy on practice problems on the marker board or PowerPoint slide. While they are working on these problems, effective teachers can continue to prepare the students for the day's activities while all the students are settled in the classroom.

This also gives time for effective teachers to take the role or see who arrived in class and take care of any miscellaneous tasks. This will also be a good use of the time that could be accomplished on minor manners that would be lost. Provide a focus for the class while the teacher can get ready to go over the exercises given on the board or PowerPoint slide.

Some teachers carry out these routines before preparing the class and once class starts; they go over this exercise, which leads to the day's lessons. Using various techniques and strategies to ensure maximum learning time such as the one given above can help being better at effective teaching. This should help maximize instructional time and the student's time on task.

Effective teachers follow a consistent schedule and maintain procedures and routines throughout every year. They also quickly handle administrative tasks, prepare materials in advance, make smooth transitions, maintain interest and momentum across lessons, and limit interruptions through behavioral management techniques.

Clear and consistent focus on achievement expectations is critical to academic success. Effective teachers believe the best for their students and expect all of them learn.

It does not matter what their skill is and where they start. They believe their students can learn; and, with great effort, students do take the time to learn. the self-fulling prophecy works both ways. If a teacher believes the students are not performing adequately, are not reachable, are not able to learn, then research must be done to find out what the problem is all about.

The expectations a teacher holds for students whether it is consciously or subconsciously is demonstrated by his or her interactions with students during instruction. Students normally found in the bottom third of the class receive lower expectations to achieve and less encouragement from many teachers. On the other side are the students in the top third of the class where teachers end up focusing their attention and giving encouragement. These negative patterns of behavior on the educator's part can be eliminated through self-observation and self-awareness. Attention and encouragement should be given to all students.

Effective teachers' expectations have been shown to relate to student achievement through high expectations for student success and towards continuous improvement. They also express and clarify expectations for student achievement as well as stress responsibility and accountability for meeting those expectations. However, to meet those expectations there needs to be a plan and a preparation for instruction.

As mentioned before, organizing time and preparing materials ahead of time for instruction has been noted as critical aspects of effective teaching. We can also think of them as broader components of the broader practice of planning carefully. By developing plans, effective teachers follow instructional or lesson plans while adjusting to fit the needs of different students.

During their planning time, effective teachers recall preconceptions and misconceptions about the subject matter itself. Taking the time for pre-assessments can help gauge students' prior knowledge of the material. Effective teachers take into account the abilities of their students as well as their strengths and weaknesses including their interest levels.

To further assist in meeting individual needs, effective teachers plan a blending of the whole group, small group, and individual instruction. Planning instruction involves careful preparation for lessons and long-term planning to make sure coverage of the curriculum is taken care of. Student achievement can be related to the amount of content coverage a teacher accomplishes. Careful planning maximizes the amount of content a teacher can cover in their lessons.

All students learn at different rates, and effective teachers can plan academic enrichment and remediation opportunities for students. Through a teacher's knowledge of the students, alternatives can be offered to a student or a small group of students who mastered the material faster than the rest of the class. Students can study the concepts at a deeper level or apply concepts differently. For those students who lack the necessary prerequisite knowledge or skills, the teacher can provide time for them to learn the foundational material before being exposed to more advanced knowledge. Make sure you provide meaningful experiences for all students to learn which should be a goal of planning.

Plan a unit that takes into account the student's prior knowledge and their learning styles. This will provide effective methods for instruction. Some teachers end up teaching in a manner that they learn best; however, this does not help the students learning the process. Effective instruction can take place beyond a comfort zone and incorporate different learning styles. Students can benefit if the material is connected to what they are already familiar with prior school experiences or real-life situations they have encountered in the past.

Planning for student instruction and engaging them is a critical component for the future success of students. Some key points to remember include identifying clear lessons and learning objectives while linking activities that can be enjoyable and interesting, planning instructional and the timing of these strategies, connect instruction to real life experiences, use graphic organizers, pictures, diagrams, and outlines for effective instructional delivery, understanding student lesson plans and different learning styles when designing lessons and above all developing objectives, questions, and activities that reflect both higher-level and lower-level cognitive skills that are appropriate for the content delivery for the entire body of students in the classroom or lecture hall.

# Chapter 4

# Instruction

The psychometric approach focuses on two ways of learning which is linguistic and logical-mathematical. Another approach to intelligence is developmental progressions. Understand that each individual is unique in the processing of skills. Student's developmental progressions differ individually and depend on the combinations of ways they process information and the tasks they are given.

Different teaching styles are required to encourage students to learn from their dominant ways of processing and building on previous successful experiences. The psychological-biological perspective of intelligence supports a multi-faceted view of intelligence. Analytical, creative, and practical are multiple forms of intelligence. Everyone learns individually. No two people have the same profile of intelligences. It takes five to six hours to permanently store specific skills in the brain. It is not a good idea to teach many skills at once that rely on the same part of the brain, as information is not retained long enough in the memory. Our brains have two memory systems, which are for ordinary facts and emotionally charged ones. Our rational thinking decreases when our emotions decrease.

Linguistic intelligence has to do with highly developed auditory skills. These are the people who enjoy reading and writing, have a good memory, spell words accurately, and use the language fluently. Teaching methods include lectures, word games, storytelling, speech, debates, reading aloud, reading, writing, spelling, and listening exercises. Those students who do not process linguistically should be taught in multidimensional ways using pictures, movement, or music.

Logical-mathematical intelligence has to do with exploring patterns and relationships, problem-solving and reasoning, following sequential logical directions, enjoys mathematics, and using experiments for testing. Teaching methods include making charts, graphs, and lists, sequencing patterns and relationships, outlining, the ability to solve problems, carrying out calculations, categorizing, questioning, and predicting.

Spatial intelligence has to do with enjoying art activities, reading maps, charts, and diagrams, doing puzzles, and thinking about pictures and images. Teaching methods include the use of pictures, diagrams, posters, slides, graphics, movies, mind maps, and colors representing words or letters.

Musical intelligence has to do with sounds from the environment, enjoying music, listening to music when studying, singing songs, and tapping rhythms. Teaching methods include chanting, clapping or snapping fingers, poetry, moving rhythmically, and music that matches the curriculum. Music engages students in the learning process through the emotional and rational parts of the brain.

Body-kinesthetic intelligence has to do with processing information through their bodies, requiring hands-on learning, being well-coordinated, using the body in skilled ways, and acting things out. Teaching methods includes manipulatives, simulations, games hands-on activities, and laboratory experiments. Remember for longterm memory to take place for students, who use the bodily-kinesthetic methods, the brain must be activated through movement.

Naturalist intelligence has to do with recognizing and classifying scientific phenomena, hearing sounds from the environment, enjoying being outdoors and interacting with the environment. Students use certain combinations of bits of intelligence to carry out different tasks.

Interpersonal intelligence helps individuals recognize and understand the differences about other individuals' feelings and intentions. Students show this intelligence when they interact in small groups and with the teacher. Intrapersonal intelligence helps individuals to distinguish their feelings, build models of themselves and draw on these models to make decisions about their lives. Students need to be able to understand their strengths and weaknesses and the kind of decisions they make.

Understand individuals vary what they learn and the information presented in the material. All categories of intelligence can be developed to its fullest potential when combined with different categories. I have found that when students are engaged in the learning process, they do not misbehave. Educators who use multiple forms of intelligence can encourage students to engage their strengths that translate from one intelligence to another. Remember that not all students learn the same way on the same day.

Psychological, biological, social, and environmental factors contribute to the learning process. Students can be taught how to translate from dominant intelligences to their less dominant intelligence. Once students feel they are succeeding in learning the material, then they are willing to try harder.

Personalize instruction to accommodate how students learn. Combining different parts of the brain helps students process the information easier. If we do not teach each individual the correct way to process the information, then we cannot see the potential each student can achieve. Each student can develop multiple intelligences through several different ways of learning.

We can think of reflective thinking based on it being interior and exterior. Interior reflective thinking has to do with perception, constructing a knowledge base, values and principles, creativity, persistence, task commitment, and communication skills. Exterior reflective thinking involves observing the class and the behavior of students, helping student's needs, gathering new information, looking into various strategies and perspectives clarifies values, prioritize goals, set standards, and synthesizes ideas. Exterior reflective thinking also involves taking appropriaterisks concentrate on goals, overcomes problems to complete goals, organizes ideas, has active listening skills, resolves conflict, and monitors oneself.

Essential knowledge and skills for educators include teaching skills and techniques, interpersonal skills, knowledge of oneself and the students, knowledge of the subject matter, knowledge of educational theory and research, problem-solving, and reflection.

Essential skills for successful teaching in a diverse society include the ability to communicate with students from different cultures, accessing abilities of students in other cultures, reassessing one's own culture's attitudes, values, and beliefs. Being able to respond in a positive way and in a sensible way to the diversity of behavior in multicultural settings, knowledge about the impact of prejudice and racism, inquiries about multicultural issues, understanding that people are more alike than different, and an appreciation of a diverse society is needed to be successful at teaching in a diverse society.

A teacher's preparation, professional relationships with students, and classroom management are all linked together for success in the classroom setting and to further carry out instruction. After the instruction is planned and the classroom is prepared, effective teachers should begin to interact with the students and with the curriculum of material being taught. Strategies, clarity of the material being presented, and kinds of questions being asked are all important factors. Methods to keep the students focused and engaged are important in implementing instruction effectively.

A repertoire of teaching strategies is needed for overall effectiveness. They need to be successfully implemented in the context and instructional goals. Students who have teachers that develop and regularly integrate inquiry-based, hands-on learning activities, critical thinking skills and assessments in their daily lessons outperform their peers. You should also be flexible and adapt using a variety of teaching strategies that contribute to effective teaching. Effective teachers are constantly searching for group instructional strategies that are just as effective as one-on-one tutoring.

Effective teachers who use a range of strategies ends up reaching more students because they tap into more different learning styles and interests students have. Different strategies should be used to ensure concepts are well understood. Use instructional techniques that involve individual, small group, and whole-class instruction. This allows effective teachers to monitor and pace their instruction based on the needs of their students.

Some strategies and activities that seem effective promoting student achievement includes direct teaching and guided independent problem-solving. Using manipulative models combined with an integrated approach in probem solving improves students' performance. Using concept mapping, graphing organizers, pictures, and diagrams promote understanding and retention. Effective teachers note problem-solving in the curriculum as being important for the success of their students.

Have students apply basic principles in their lessons. Effective teachers stress how important higher mental processes are such as creativity, problem-solving techniques, and analytical thinking skills. Having these skills enable students to relate learning to real-life situations and incorporate concepts into long-term memory. It also does not hurt to include student ideas and elicits student comments on how to improve instruction.

In other words, techniques and instructional strategies have as much influence on student learning as the aptitude of a student. Lecturing has always been a common strategy, but there has always been a need to quickly cover the material and overload students with data that cannot always be processed immediately.

Lecturing needs to be done effectively. I encourage hands-on learning which also correlates to student achievement. Studies show that those students who have hands-on learning activities out-perform their peers, especially in the math and sciences. Higher achievement rates happen when effective teachers use instruction with meaningful conceptualization. Effective teachers know that there is no one instructional strategy that can be used for all situations. There should be a broad spectrum of approaches to teaching that should be successful for the students.

There needs to be a communication factor and expect high expectations for students. Effective teacher's ability to give focused explanations and clarify achievements is critical aspects to effective instructional delivery. They expect students to learn and take the responsibility to make sure students do learn. They set high standards and provides a challenging curriculum for all of their students. Yes, achievement is indeed related to the range of teaching strategies teachers employ, but the clarity of explanation and expectation are separate skills promoting teaching effectiveness.

Communication is vital for any profession that requires interaction with people and the organization. It is manifested in two different ways such as explaining the content in a clear and focused manner, pointing out important concepts and relationships, and the concern the teacher's clarity explaining directions how students are to complete an activity.

Effective teachers require clear communication of expectations, encouragement, and caring. Communicating content in the teaching profession requires teachers to understand the subject matter and how to share the subject matter with students so they can understand it. There must be a climate of support and encouragement so that all students participate in the two-way teaching and learning process. Effective management and students' ability to learn are related to effective communications.

Based on past studies, effective teaching has to do with clarifying expressions, giving examples and guided practice exercises, setting high expectations, finding strategies towards improvement and growth in the classroom settings, and the student's responsibility and accountability for meeting such high expectations. The importance of teaching metacognitive strategies to help support reflection and the learning process should also be used during instruction.

Now teaching is not easy since each discipline is complex and how complex students who can learn. Effective teachers must have sufficient knowledge of subject matter and an appreciation of teaching and learning. They also recognize each student being different and being multifaceted. Each student brings a lifetime of ideas and experiences both in and out of school to classroom settings.

Effective teachers recognize classes are dynamic and complex with many different personalities. These different understandings of people are needed in to order to effectively interact with students, carrying out plans and practices for managing the place, and preparing and differentiating student learning needs. Effective teachers emphasize meaning in their instructions. They take the time to encourage students to respond to questions and activities, which require them to assimilate their own understanding rather than just memorizing the material. They also engage with students in content at different various levels using a broad spectrum of objectives that address higher and lower levels of cognitive ability.

Studies have shown that effective teaching can take place by having students learn and demonstrate understanding of the meaning of the material rather than memorizing the material; however, memorizing the material should also be carried out. Effective teachers place a high priority on reading ability since it affects the content areas and overall achievements in many other areas. Higher achievement can take place when the focus of instruction is on meaningful conceptualization, especially if the student can relate his or her own knowledge to the real world.

Questioning techniques is also proven valuable. Questions and answers from teachers to students and vice versa represent much needed academic instruction that takes place in school settings. The process itself supports student engagement in learning and the teacher's ability to monitor students' progress. Both lower level and higher-level questions are needed to encourage student achievement.

Questions tend to be more valuable when they receive appropriate responses, and these responses encourage student engagement to demonstrate whether they understand the material or not. Both the level of difficulty and cognitive level of questions should reflect the contents and the goal of the lessons. It needs to be interesting where students can be involved with sufficient variance type across lessons to maintain interest and momentum.

Specific questions should be considered carefully and be prepared in advance for lessons to make sure they support the goals and emphasize key points as well as maintaining an appropriate level of difficulty and complexity. The questions should be considered in sequence and not as isolated units when it comes to planning, implementing and assessing student needs. Questioning techniques become critical when assessing student learning. Emphasis on wait time can be an an important component of questioning. Longer wait times for students to respond and think about the material can also demonstrate higher achievement levels, but at the same time wait, times should also be considered to maintain student engagement and lesson momentum.

It is also important to support student engagement in the learning process. Yes, time allocated to teaching, the time spent students working on their projects, and the ability to work well together leads to classroom success. Effective teachers use various strategies calling on students randomly and who are be willing to provide any additional clarification and illustration. Positive reinforcement, praising students, and employing meaningful activities helps students achieve the ability to learn more and be comfortable with their teachers.

There should be appropriate learning activities and appropriate questioning for the clarity and explanation of both contents and directions. Effective teachers are always accepting, supportive, and continue to be persistent at challenging and engaging students during aspects of instruction. They vary their instructional strategies, their types of assignments and activities given to the students to increase student's engagement in their lessons.

Student's ability to interact one-on-one with the teacher tends to be higher if there is an interest in learning the material. Carrying out systematic directions for procedures has shown to help students learn the material better. I have found most of my students learn the material much faster. Successful student engagement with real-life activities of interest makes the social and learning atmosphere more positive. A lot of excellent teaching skills, activities, and articles can also be found by studying teaching journals. There are many journals out there, and I encourage you to find your favorite journal to continue and keep current in your teaching profession.

# Chapter 5

# Techniques Part 1

Let us now look at some techniques of instruction. Taking the time to monitor and assess student development and work is not an easy task. Homework even at the university level should still be encouraged for most courses even when some students participate in so many outside activities. Some teachers become frustrated with students who do not complete homework assignments. Homework is an effective part of teaching even when I have been tutoring my clients as a private tutor.

One of the most influential factors contributing to student learning is the amount of time spent doing homework. We can think of homework as practice, preparation, patience, and promoting to do excellent work. Practicing homework assignments reinforces familiar concepts that should be refined. Preparing for homework exercises exposes students to concepts that they will need to study in-depth for the next class session. Exploring and learning the concepts is what is needed for mastery of the content of the material.

Effective teachers establish guidelines such as the purpose of the assignment, the amount of homework that will be assigned, expectations for completing the homework, and any assistance that is required. They also share guidelines to communicate them to the students and parents. Think of the teacher, the program, and the parent forming a triangle with the student at the exact center. Based on this triad, all three factors at the corners of the triangle have the best and greatest contact with the student.

Effective teachers do not assume parents will always be supportive of doing homework. They provide students with the right tools to make homework successful. It is important to find a space to do homework in bright light, establish a time for the homework to be done effectively, and have parents ask what is being taught during the school day and what needs to be done each night. It is good for parents to explain the benefits of doing homework and if there need to be lots of coaching needed.

When teachers give parents, ideas on how to help and support their children, both the homes and schools become more connected and strengthened. Homework experience becomes more productive. Effective teachers assign homework, check it, and bad review it regularly. Teachers who spend time giving homework and providing considerable supportive feedback make higher and better gains than those students who fail to spend time not doing homework. I remember taking the time to write so much detail grading homework, quizzes, and tests and writing a lot of feedback. My students found it to be incredibly helpful.

By continuing to provide feedback, the ability to learn the material increases along the way. However, keep in mind it is also the quality and the quantity of the homework that is considered important. Homework that provides thought for subsequent use in class discussions or writing activities become more beneficial. This empowers students to learn but only if they complete the homework.

Effective teachers grade papers whether it is homework, quizzes, or tests to measure students learning the process. Nevertheless, most educators take a long time to grade papers. Grading papers quicker can be achieved by formatting answers into either short phrases, nonsense words, or even a story. Not all-multiple choice questions need to have the traditional letters A, B, C, and D but encompass all letters of the alphabet A - Z. Besides grading papers side by side when grading or if possible have only one sheet of a test that can adjusted for all of the questions can also be time-efficient.

Effective teachers provide goals and guidelines for homework and allow students to use those requirements such as in performances, creative writing assignments, or possibly videotapes. They use homework as the primary tool to assess learning needs for a wide range of students in their classrooms. It is given that homework has positive effects on student achievement, and when it is graded, commented on, and discussed in the next class lesson.

Assessment is the main component in the teaching process. It was used to determine how effective the lesson based on student learning and student engagement, evaluate student progress, and for continuing to improve instruction. They provide feedback on what strategies are working, which students need more assistance, and if the content needs to be revised. Addressing areas of weakness in the subject the matter is critical for effective teaching and improving student's scores.

Effective teachers use a variety of assessment practices to monitor all types of student learning which includes formal and informal assessments as well as formative and summative assessments. They take the time to monitor students' progress informally using techniques such as scanning and circulating the room. It can also be as simple as talking to individuals or a group of students about tasks and activities. They also make notes about difficulties they observe thinking of what they can do to improve student scores and to better reach out to students. Formal monitoring of student progress includes giving out quizzes and tests, projects, or writing assignments. Using assessments works for both individuals and groups of students.

Effective teachers use fair tests that relate to the material they were teaching. They understand how to interpret the information from standardized and teacher-made tests. Counting how many students missed the same questions and then analyzing those questions to determine if they were misleading or if the students did not learn the material at all is a technique teachers can use. Teaching test-taking skills can also assist students to score higher on quizzes and examinations.

Effective teachers can group questions by concepts they are assessing and determine if the entire concept should be retaught with different instructional approaches. They follow up on their assessments by re-teaching the material and providing more enrichment as needed. They need to make sure that they are aligned with the curriculum and when actual instruction that takes place.

Many educators recognize feedback to students based on their work. It is a powerful technique for increasing learning outcomes for students. They provide feedback in a timely manner, and they make sure it relates to the criteria at a task. The amount of time between the activity and the feedback is critical to student achievement. It is not a good idea to delay giving feedback. It is less likely for students to respond to the feedback, and it is very likely that learning will not be enhanced.

Effective teachers provide feedback that needs to be corrective. It is not a good idea to indicate just right and wrong answers since this can have a negative impact on student learning. They provide specific explanations on what students are doing correctly and what they are not doing correctly and how to fix it. Students need to take the time to critically evaluate their work and provide constructive criticism to others.

Students should be provided the parameters of success before working on their assignments. They should then assess their own work before submitting it to their teacher. Offering the students an opportunity to get feedback and then resubmit their work for additional credit is worthwhile and reinforces revisions and the learning process. Getting feedback from oneself, their peers, and the teacher enhances the learning process.

Effective teachers use inputs to monitor student progress and they collect information from learners who they work in class using techniques such as mental notes, work samples and feedback should assist the teacher creating improved meanings of instruction for students.

Again, effective teachers in schools use pre-assessments to support targeted teaching of skills to learn material better, implement strong monitoring strategies by asking questions related to the objectives of the lessons, choose information sources they use for assessing learning needs, monitor students for signs of misconceptions, give timely feedback, show support and encouragement, reteach students who did not achieve mastery, and even provide additional tutoring for those who seek additional help.

It is also important to respond to a range of student needs. Effective teachers know how to recognize individual and group differences among their students and be able to accommodate those differences when carrying out their instruction. They need to adapt instruction to meet student needs, which requires careful assessment and planning for students in the classroom. They also need to select from a wide range of strategies to find the best match for the context being taught.

Successful teachers present information where the The majority of the class can be challenged and are successful. They adapt assignments that meet other student needs who are both higher and lower functioning or who need to present the material differently. Teaching study and organizational skills have also been effective. Improvising while teaching to meet the learning needs of students is another sign of an effective teacher. Specialized training working with a broad range of students such as a diverse group of a body of students, gifted students, and special need students also make an effective teacher.

Using scaffolding approaches to instruction allows students to get the help they need to work at the own pace. The use of many resources such as content area specialists, other students, family members, volunteers, tutors, community members, conferences, and seminars to meet the needs of students are all-available for teachers to use effective teaching methods.

Again, students are more likely engaged and achieve the most success when instruction matches their achievement level and needs. Students who participate in development training for implementing instruction have students with higher learning outcomes. Effective teachers have a variety of grouping strategies with differentiation to support student learning. A different type of instruction requires careful monitoring and assessment of student progress.

There should still be that factor of proper management and proper behavior in the classroom. A group student with similar needs for instruction has also been effective. Effective teachers understand their students as individuals based on abilities, achievement, learning styles, and their needs. Demonstrating excellence in teaching with a full range of students makes an effective teacher. Do not stay satisfied with current accomplishments by developing a plan for growth. Growth helps you lead. The better you are, the more people who will listen to you and the greater your value and the greate the potential for tomorrow.

If you are going to make the most of your talent at teaching, then know that nothing is interesting if you do not feel interested. Those people who are successful view learning differently from those who are not successful. Learning should be a passion, and you should be able to value people. Be able to develop relationships with growth potential. Choose a mentor to help you grow. If you are going to be successful at teaching and to be aleader, you need to be able to find the strength zones where people do best.

If you are going to form a team of people, you have to get to know the people on your team, communicate to your team to see how they fit on the team and emphasize zero competition. Deciding the people on the team who are worth equipping and developing is a stepping-stone to building a better team. Empower team members with responsibility and authority. Give credit for the team's success. Give the team the chance to succeed. Those closest to the leader determine the success of the leader.

Great teachers seek out, find potential teachers, and then transform them into great teachers. Characteristics to look for in a leader include character, influence, positive attitude, excellent people skills, talent, a great record of accomplishment, confidence, self-discipline, excellent communication skills.

According to John C Maxwell, steps to being a great leader include model, mentor, monitor, motivate, and multiply. Training requires responsibility, authority, and accountability. You need to be able to value your team members. Leaders value what their team members' value, add value to their team members, and make themselves more valuable.

If you are going to enlarge your team members, believe in others before they start believing in you, be able to serve others before they serve you, add value to other people before they add value to you. People will always move towards someone who increases them. You need to have the right people in the right places to be a success for everyone.

Remember leadership involves influence, priorities, integrity, making positive changes, positive attitudes, self-discipline, problem-solving, and developing people. You can be better tomorrow as both an educator and a leader than you are today. The best leaders in the middle make better leaders at the top by directing their influences up higher leaders, down to their students, and across with their colleagues and co-workers.

# Chapter 6

# Techniques Part 2

Student grades seem to be important. Those little letters educators assign make powerful presentations about one's academic performance. They are critical to one's life earning potential, your employment, and your self-image. When it comes to teaching students to get better grades, some people find it difficult to believe if it can be done or not for those who consistently fail. Henry Ford one time stated, "If you think you can do well in school, you're right. If you don't think you can do well in school, you're still right."

Let us start thinking right about how we can teach students. If we are going to teach well, we need to start thinking the right way. Start thinking positive and avoid that internal critic inside you telling you cannot do it. You can succeed in the teaching profession. I want you to start teaching the smart way instead of teaching the hard way.

If two people were given the task to write something on paper where one person had a pencil and the other person had a stick, you can see the person with the pencil will accomplish more and write something. The person using the stick will not accomplish anything. The person using the pencil is teaching the smart way and not working extra hard to write something using only a stick.

When it comes to teaching at the college level or university level, do know that these places are big business. Understand that students are investing time, money, and their future life expectations. Use effective tools of teaching such as using computers, copy machines, marker boards, overhead projectors, and PowerPoint slides. Never miss a class to teach that otherwise many students will suffer. It is a good idea to have a backup professor to fill in the position just in case you cannot teach for particular days.

Tell your students about the courses that they like to take. After all, they are spending a lot of money to invest in their education. If they choose the subjects they like, then they will do the best in these subjects and they will be best for them.

We end up doing best at the things we like to do, and if you like teaching and if it is a passion, then you will do well. I never listen to other people that tell me that specific courses are hard or even hard to teach. I have had students who never took a course in chemistry and have walked out achieving high grades at the end of the semester.

It does not hurt to check out other professors before they test other students. Excellent professors can choose to make a course interesting and enjoyable. A terrible professor can make an interesting course awful if it is not taught well. If you want to teach well to your students, then know you and allow them to sit in your classes to see how allow them to see you as one of the best professors in the school setting. Have students meet with you and get to it is like.

Eventually, students will talk about their opinions and the professors they choose. Students seem to keep a record of their impressions and their responses. I recommend selecting courses you like to teach as well as select students who you like to teach. The students who like and respect you will also encourage you to be their teacher or professor.

I remember one of my second private students kept encouraging me to be her tutor as she saw faith in learning the material and my ability to teach. Towards the end of the semester, I learned by surprise she was accepted into the university of her choice. She saw something special about me as a person and as a past professor who never gave up. She never gave up on me despite lacking some confidence, and I never gave up on her. It may also be a good idea to carry cards about your experiences with students as references to how well you taught.

Most of the best educators in teaching get the most out of reading the books they enjoy. Get your textbooks before teaching the classes and read them as soon as possible. You want to start the quarter or semester on the right foot. We all know reading can be more interesting when you do not have to read it and when there is no deadline to meet. Once you start teaching, it is harder to sit back and read something you have not had time to read. Unpressured reading of the material before teaching can be enjoyable.

Regardless of what subject is being taught, all students need to have strong reading skills. To enhance reading comprehension, do your best to read aloud to simulate the right or visual and left or verbal sides of your brain. Let us take a closer look at the right and left sides of the brain. Scientific fields are constantly making discoveries. Just like our muscles, it is the other part of the body we can develop. If we do not actively use it, it will waste away if it is not used properly. We need to get our students to exercise their brains just as much as we exercise and build the rest of their bodies.

Understand the right hemisphere of our brains governs the artistic, musical, imaginative, and innovative portions of our thoughts. The left hemisphere controls the analytical, mathematical, scientific, and logical thoughts that we think. The student who uses both sides of his or her brain becomes the most successful in either profession that use either the right or left-brains. Our dreams and insights into the world around us also contribute to the right brain functions. If we consider these ideas and be creative about them, then we may come up with answers from out of nowhere.

Have students develop their right and left-brains. If your students are mostly left-brained and are into the math and sciences, they also have them learn about right brain activities such as music, art, or theater. That does not mean they should enroll in these courses which they may not achieve the highest grade possible but they can learn them at the side.

Those students who are right-brain can watch scientific shows found on PBS. I have found the shows to be well done that even the right brain person will find them to be entertaining, informative, and interesting. I find educational programming great for both types of students. They provide great mental workouts and increase knowledge in almost every academic subject. I have found professors who are left-brain will be rigid in their grading policies and might listen to logic and reason. However, the right brain professor's grading scale is more flexible and you may have a better chance of negotiating with other people in your life.

Have students get ahead start reading the material, and even have them over study the material as if they can continue to repeat the material in their sleep. Once students start their courses, they can then level off at an easier pace. Teach students to have rigorous study habits, help, and coach them along the way to achieve the highest grades as possible. Successful praise can be the best motivator. Once they feel successful, it is hard to give up. Allow students to build confidence so that there higher education becomes enjoyable and so they can take pride in their earned accomplishments.

If you are going to be effective in your ability to teach students, then you need to be there for them. Never miss a chance to help them when they need it. This is reflected in my teaching whether it was in K-12, the college level, or private tutoring. The less chances I had helping my students, the higher grades they achieved, and it are also similar to students who attend classes. The less classes they miss, the chances of succeeding is higher versus those who miss many classes.

Also, keep in mind that the first and last minutes of teaching are sometimes the most important periods of teaching. Important information is sometimes given during these announcement periods whether there will be an upcoming quiz or test or even relevant information needed to do well on the next quiz or test. Of course, if your students miss class, then have them get notes from someone else. Furthermore, never miss a class, do not leave early, and above all do not leave late.

Let us now picture our students in the classroom setting. You are teaching them the subject matter of your profession. For them to learn the material, they need to take effective notes. For you to teach them well, they need to know how to take notes effectively.

One of the techniques I use is using a special kind of green paper where there is a vertical line about one-third way from the left edge of the paper. On the left side is where I have my students write the topics, subtopics, and questions for the lessons. On the other side is where I have them take notes. When it comes time for studying the material, I advise them to cover the second half of twothirds of the paper and quiz themselves what they learned based on the topics, subtopics, or questions on the left hand side.

Have students take notes with a purpose. The purpose of taking notes is to study and learn the material from class. Students are also encouraged to take notes from the readings in their courses, which I referred to them as text notes. Always use key words and find the main idea when having students write their notes from the textbook. It is best students write text notes based on the same information presented from the teaching material. This is also an effective way to teach students and have them learn the material better.

When students mark up books, they tend to highlight so many sentences. I'm not saying this is not a good idea, but I will say it is more effective to use a pencil to mark only the parts you are not sure about or simply do not know. In other words, make notes of material you do not know in the textbook.

Have students come with their own set of exam questions. This is what we do as educators to test the material presented in class. They will seem more prepared and score higher if they are thinking actively in the process. Studies have shown that students score higher by being active in this learning process. You may even have students also use their notes to make up questions the teacher is going to test them on.

Another technique is to take your notes and draw a line down the center of a sheet. Use the left side for key points from the textbook, and use the right side to add any key points you the educator want to teach the students. This way you can compare the similarities what is being taught and fill in any details on either side of the sheet to clear up misunderstandings.

When studying your notes, it is a waste of time to spend a lot of time pouring over them. It is far more effective to study notes over short periods rather than studying them over long periods. We learn more by studying in short intervals with more first and last important points of learning material. Again, study in short sessions with short breaks in between.

After class is over, immediately review your lecture notes but spend time alone for yourself. If that does not work, then study with your friends and/or other tutors. They may be able to spot mistakes, point out concepts you may have not known, make up new questions that others may not have thought of, and even answer questions you do not know.

You must review your lecture notes immediately and if not the same day. Concepts seem to build up as each day progresses. If there is something you do not understand, then immediately have your students seek help from you as the professor to get things cleared up. Waiting a week or two before the next big test can be a nightmare and turn out to be a probable failure for the student to learn the material. It might be too late to learn a huge amount of material. Getting concepts cleared up and having your students finish their homework on time can make a big difference.

Effective teachers or professors when teaching their classes can also give extra credit, but should also let their students know that extra credit should never be optional. Have students never miss extra credit work. In reality, it is not extra if everyone is allowed to do it. It could mean the difference between an A- and a B+. It can make a difference in the final grade of a student. Have them make a habit to complete any small projects necessary to get the work done.

Have students pretest themselves using old study guides, old quizzes, old tests, or even supplements you might suggest. Have them get as much recommended materials in addition to the ones they may already have. There are plenty of bookstores, libraries, or even friends who have taken the course and who may be available to assist you. You could have them build a file on quizzes and exams.

Some teachers and professors understand that their quizzes and exams are circulated so they do not allow them to keep their quizzes or exams. I recommend that after they take their quizzes and exams, immediately find a quiet spot for themselves to write down what they recalled was on the exam. Writing down important topics and questions and building a file on it can make a huge difference for the success for several students.

Effective teachers or professors can also help students become expert test takers. The best thing to do is to keep practicing taking tests. Your students can increase their test taking skills by even taking short tests in magazines, newspapers, puzzle books, or even watching game shows. The more you practice anything in life; eventually you will get better at it. Understand that the number of questions examiners test on is limited. This is always the case. Most questions appear and reappear on later tests or variations used in earlier tests. Take the time to become acquainted with the structure of the tests. You heard the saying that practice makes perfect.

Effective educators can also teach about educated guessing. Here are some techniques you can share when students answer multiple-choice questions. If there are two out of the four choices as being opposites, then pick one of those two choices as the best guess. The answers B, C, and D are usually but not always the best in five answer multiple-choice questions. Sometimes, it is okay when the same letter for each answer choice is the same. No answer choices can be possible, but can also be poor guess choices.

When questions ask about the most or least choices, pick the answer next to the most or least choice. Some answers include all of the above as answer choices, which is also a good guess. Long multiple-choice answers are also good answer choices. However, be careful when the answer choice mixes half true and half-false answers, then the whole answer is false.

If there are two out of the four answer choices that are almost identical, it is probably best to pick the answer choice that is the longer of the two. If there are only a few questions that have more than four answer choices, then it might be best to choose one of the the last few answers choices.

Choose answers in the correct tense whether it is singular or plural. Limiting words such as never, all, always, and must are usually false. General terms such as most, some, usually, might, and could are usually true answer choices. Watch out for exaggerated or complex answer choices because they are generally false. Identify answers with a tick mark at the side to the questions you are not sure about, and come back to answer those questions again.

For fill-in-the-blank questions, it is a good idea not to leave a question blank. You may guess the answer correctly, and if you do not get it right, you may get partial credit. When writing essay exams, write as much as you can by writing short paragraphs. Be sure to write legibly because volume, quality, clarity, and of course neatness makes a difference.

It is also a good idea to reread directions before you turn in an exam, and use the entire period to double-check your answers. Some answers do pop up in other questions. First impression answers are usually the best guesses. If you find a question difficult to visualize, then do take the time to draw it out.

Come up with your answer and work backwards to see if you are right. I always recommend my students to sit in the front row of the class or towards the front because you end up paying attention more. Ambiguous questions can be cleared up when you are sitting closer to the teacher or professor. Stay until the end of the class when the teacher or professor might clarify questions. Remember the first few minutes and the last few minutes of class are important since valuable information might be given.

Let us talk now about writing effective papers and how we can teach that to our students. It makes sense to have students never turn in homework that is late, sloppy, or not edited. Writing clear and concise expressions is essential for school and life afterwards. Find a trusted person to proofread your material. Always take the time to have your students perfect their papers on a word processor. First impressions count and if that cover sheet is not impressive, then it is likely no one is going to even want to open the page and read the rest of the essay.

Think of written work as a comparison between different papers among the students in the classroom. Reinforce that just about every paper should be proofread and appearance makes all the difference in the world. We can think of five different steps to better writing. The first step is coming up with an outline. Build from the central idea to several topics and then add details to each of those topics.

You now have your main idea, which is your central idea in your introduction of your paper. Each topic is the main idea sentence in the rest of the paragraphs, and the details are the detail sentences for each paragraph. Having this information, you can carry out the second step and write a sentence outline. If you are working on your paper on the computer, then you can leave space in between paragraphs to add or delete any material needed. This is what I call the third step in the writing process.

The fourth step involves building on the ideas you came up with and refine sentences to make them more creative and interesting. If you need to keep carrying out more modifications for the essay, then do so until it becomes complete. More additional sentences can be added to illustrate or explain the meaning of the topic sentences in your paragraphs.

The final step is to polish the essay. Take time to check your work for grammar, spelling, trite words or phrases, and repetition that is not needed. It does not hurt to read the entire article aloud to yourself and a trusted person. Have a trusted friend proofread your student's paper, but make sure they do not write it for them. The chances are your students have written a paper that will be a winner as long as you the educator have met all guidelines.

At this point, if you want to get your name out there and be that popular excellent professor, then have students take advantage of registration tricks. Have them register on time and do not wait until the last minute. The best courses with the best professors fill up fast. Some students get discouraged if they cannot get into the class they want with that excellent professor. It is not the end of the world as there are so many other opportunities in life out there.

Let students know that at many schools, some students students drop out of the class, fail to pay the required fees, or even lack the necessary perquisites. Also, have them keep in mind that registering again may not be an alternative. Never give up letting students into your course if you think they can succeed. The best professors often find ways to make room for persistent and interested students. Do not put all your trust in one person out there when making decisions whether it is in the teaching profession or in life. Some students probably even memorize the course catalog as a way to keep track of the courses they plan to take.

Effective teaching consists of students understanding of the subject, applying what they have learned in new situations, and a desire to continue learning many new things. Effective educators use different models of teaching based on student learning, child development, and the ability to think, and peer mediation.

Learning should be viewed as the acquisition of new behaviors. Being able to model, carry out constructivism, and scaffolding is based on how students construct meaning what they have learned. Cognitive processes of learning include information processing, inquiry learning, and discovery learning. Peer-mediated instruction has to do with learning taking place in social situations. It includes cooperative learning, group investigation, and peer-age and cross-age tutoring.

Effective teaching focuses on outcomes. These outcomes include goals, objectives, and performance tasks. Educators should be able to modify their instruction based on the assessment of understanding the material. Measuring which refers to gathering data related to their student's knowledge and skills and evaluating the outcomes is needed. Traditional tests and the use of assessments can be used to measure and evaluate student learning.

# Chapter 7

# Techniques Part 3

Let us talk about memory techniques. Memory is a great tool to save both time and energy. Almost everything that we do in our daily lives is based on memory and our ability to recall. I have found that memory strategies used by students are not used very effectively. Take time to commit ideas to memory when you are well-rested. Do not memorize material when you are tired. You will have difficulty learning and comprehending the material.

I teach students to learn material in short sessions rather than one long session. The first and last items of learning material are easier to recall when concentration is at its peak. Breaking up an hour session into three twenty-minute intervals gives more first and last periods of recall learning the material. Memory consists of concentration and observation, repetition, and association.

As a past biochemistry major with an emphasis in chemistry, I had the chance to learn more about biological molecules and molecules such as vitamins. Certain vitamins can help improve your memory quite a bit. It is important to eat well and supplement your diet with the following vitamins. Vitamin C protects nerve tissue. If you have too little Vitamin C it can lead to mental confusion. Vitamin B-1 is also called thiamine. It produces energy for nerve cells in the brain. Vitamin B-3 is also called niacin that helps with concentration. Vitamin B-6 builds proteins from amino acids. Not having enough Vitamin B-6 leads to a lack of concentration.

Vitamin B-12 contains folic acid and iron, which prevents anemia and can lead to difficulty in concentration. It is also found that lecithin and choline are critical for memory. Finally, tyrosine is an amino acid that helps longterm memory. As long as it is okay with your primary physician, many people can benefit from having a balanced diet, which includes milk, whole-wheat bread, fish, fruits, and vegetables that contain vitamins.

Another memory technique is using acronyms. Acronyms are a group of letters, which are usually the first letters of other words. When I teach scientific notation to students enrolled in my chemistry courses forgiven large or small numbers and converting them to scientific notation, I used the acronym LIP, which stands for left, is positive. If that is the case, then right has to be negative. This allows the correct number to have the proper integer for the power often given a number in standard form.

Even rhyming strategies can help with memory recall those link ideas together. Linking ideas together is a quick way to remember long lists of unrelated ideas. If you make up a story associating each word with other words, you have a better chance of recalling the ideas. Taking key words of given material and turning them around into a funny story can help recall and learn the material better. Another way memorizing material is to use keywords, which you have already memorized and tie them to things they recall or even linking words to numbers and then linking these phrases to unrelated phrases to recall difficult material to be memorized.

Associate keywords with numbers. Looking at pictures that have a hidden number of representations can also help recall and learn the material faster. If it sounds funny, you will have a better idea of remembering it. Remember taking time to teach memory techniques in any profession can save both time and energy and be a powerful way to learn material faster and more efficient.

Excellent teaching can also be effective if we teach students to manage their time more effectively. I have found with the students who I teach that they have some obstacles to maintain excellent grades in school. Some students have to work while going to school to pay for books, tuition, and any other necessary expenses.

Some student's grade point average tends to drop because they spend a lot of time working and less time studying. Perhaps students can obtain interest-free loans to minimize the amount of time working during the school year. It also might be a good idea to save money from summer jobs to minimize the amount of time during the school year. Even turn your hobbies into small part-time businesses that may lead to some income potential. Earning potential is endless. You just have to use your imagination and the potential of the abilities you can do in your everyday life.

So at this point, we have done everything we could do to help our students achieve the best possible grade. However, there comes a time when we need to make a hard the decision between borderline grades such as being between an A, a B, even a B, or a C. I look at other factors such as attendance, effort, and my interaction with the student who constantly and consistently seek the help they need without giving up. I also take the time to look back at my quizzes and tests to see if they were consistent to what I wanted to teach the students in the class.

If you are going to teach effectively, the only way students are going to maximize their grades is for them to study based on their biological clocks. Determine when your students are going to study their best. Some people prefer studying early in the morning, which I consider them as early birds, whereas other people prefer studying late at night, which again I consider them as night owls. Then there are groups of people who are somewhere between early birds and night owls. We tend to concentrate on the best of our abilities when our temperatures are the highest.

Taking the time to teach our students how to studycan also maximize their grades. Mastering how to study effectively has always been a proven success. Actively reviewing the material is much more efficient than passively reviewing the material. During the active review process, we take the time to go through the material and ask potential exam questions and then take the time to practice writing those answers as we would on a test. Francis P. Robinson was a renowned educator who came up with the method called SQ3R, which stands for Survey, The question, Read, Recite, and Review. I use the method called the PQRST method, which stands for Preview, The question, Read, Self-Recite, and Test. It was a variation to help Air Force officers improve their studies. I have found this method to be incredibly valuable during the art of my excellent teaching. I always have my students preview each page of the book, then take the boldface title and subtitles, and turn them around into questions. This helps in the active process learning the material better and thinking about the possible answers to the questions based on the titles and subtitles.

Of course, then there is the reading portion. But I tell them to use speed reading techniques such as reading in phrases and staring in the middle of the page and moving your eyes left to right as you visualize and comprehend what your reading. Effective skills in reading is powerful to get students to learn the material faster and more efficient versus someone who would spend months passively reading the material and getting nowhere. Nevertheless, remember what we talked about earlier they will need to relate what they have read to real-life experiences for them to bring the learning process to long-term memory.

The self-recitation is the most powerful technique above all letters in the PQRST method. Taking time to recite the material is more efficient to the learning process than simply passive reading where we tend to forget what we read. If students can teach themselves what they have read, then they have learned the material. If they cannot, then all they did was exercise their eyes reading from left to right or if they are from other countries who read from right to left or from top to bottom. Either way, the process is just a waste of time. Self-reciting the material is not easy, but with patience and practice, it can be done.

The last letter in PQRST is the T, which again stands for a test. Taking the time to answer questions at the end of each section or chapter is a great way to check your understanding of the material. You heard the saying at the gym. No pain leads to any gain.

Another method is the Four Steps to Mastery or abbreviated as 4S = M. The first step is the preliminary survey. This is where students recall yesterdays' assignment and relate it to a new assignment. Reading headings, summary paragraphs, and study questions is part of this method. The second step is to read for ideas. Turn the readings of what you are learning into questions where you can answer them yourself.

The third step is to retrace the steps the students went through by skimming to look for the main ideas. The fourth and last step is to write a summary that contains the information found in the assignment. If there is no time to write down anything, at least have students recite the material mentally.

The third step is to retrace the steps the students went through by skimming to look for the main ideas. The fourth and last step is to write a summary that contains the information found in the assignment. If there is no time to write down anything, at least have students recite the material mentally.

However, there comes a point in students ability to learn cannot be done all by themselves in courses such as the natural and agricultural sciences and engineering. I have found having students studying in groups for those who want to learn has been effective. It is like learning a new language. You can learn and comprehend faster by reading, reciting, and listening.

It is always a good idea to study in bright light. Never study in the dark since it is hard on the eyes. It can also reduce depression since we tend to be more depressed in dark natural settings. Full concentration is needed to study effectively. Reduce background noise and stay away from environments where there are many distractions.

Studies have shown that poor concentration has to do with avoidance. The more we avoid doing something, the more likely we are running away from something we probably do not want to do. Even wearing a pleasant perfume or a nice smelling cologne when studying or taking a test can also improve our chances of scoring higher on tests. As long as you are not allergic to aromatherapy, you may want to try it.

We do not want our students to be depressed. I like to see them smile and be happy. After all, that is what I feel educators should do to make our world a better place. Smiling even if you do not feel like it works wonders on your learning attitude. Make sure it is part of your daily routine. We tend to focus on negative thoughts since most people were fed negative programming from their families and friends since childhood to be protected from the real world. They tend to have that internal critic tell them to look at the world negatively. There might be some truth to this, but there is always the other side of the coin where there are positive experiences where we can learn, grow, and enjoy the wonders the world has to offer.

Smiling like positive affirmations can fight off depression more effectively. Studies show that good feelings stimulate thought processes and release positive material in memory. If you let depression get to you, then you will end up seeing a doctor who will prescribe antidepressants and make money from you and continue to make more and more money from you, and then you will be hooked on the medication for life. You will be hooked on your medication that you will eventually have otherperiods of depression where you can get into a more deep depression and have other health problems, which will lead to more medications. It is like a domino effect until you get sick and die at an early age.

You just can't win and some doctors are out there who want to be rich and won't tell you about the success of everyday life is to carry out the basic daily tasks we learned in K-12 such as brushing our teeth at least twice a day in the morning and right before we go to bed, eating balanced meals in the morning, lunch, and dinner, exercising, and getting a good night's rest. The point is to smile and be happy and you will have better teaching experiences and succeed in the profession. Always keep a positive frame of mind in your everyday life.

Effective educators know that not all classes are going to work out for them. Never be afraid to change your environment or know that the experiences for certain days are going to be positive. It is like an investor investing in stocks and bonds. A wise investor will not keep making the same mistakes by purchasing worthless securities if no growth of money takes place.

Never be afraid to move on from one school or to another work environment if you have to. Look at it as a positive experience where there will be a place where you will succeed. I have had these experiences in the past where I came across work environments with poor management or the place seemed corrupt with awful bosses, managers, and even educators writing lies on evaluations.

It was not my fault, and I know it was not my fault when I still had high success with the students I taught. I even had some co-workers and probably some bosses who hated me doing a better job than they do, but I did not care since I wanted to do what I enjoy and that is teaching and sharing the subjects I find interesting. In fact, I have actually had past professors and teachers who actually gave me unfair letter grades and past managers and supervisors who made poor and unfair decisions who a few realize later made a mistake. We do not live in that perfect ideal world that we see on Sesame Street in childhood.

Nevertheless, that should not stop you from doing the right things in life and carry on excellent teaching. There is a lesson to the injustices in this world. We may not be able to solve all of our problems ourselves and we may not be able to bring justice to some situations at the right time and right place, but there will always be someone or some event that will bring justice and solve the injustices we faced in our past life. We may not be there to see it, but rest assured have faith it does happen. I share this because I even found the best and the top excellent teachers feel unappreciated in their teaching efforts due to the wide range of nonsense issues that goes on in the classroom setting and even in real life. If you are going to succeed in the teaching profession, be that best educator you can possibly be without letting other people let you down.

Building your personal library at home can also make you into an effective educator. I have over a thousand books from childhood from books I used in schools to books that I bought and even books that were donated to me. I have found that each author of even the same subject matter looks at things in a different way. Understanding how to teach in different learning styles as mentioned in the previous chapters helps students learn the material much better.

Even so, I still found that no matter how many different teaching styles I use and whether or not I use multiple colors on the marker board or using multiple colors using pens with multiple colors of scratch paper to teach students to make the material interesting, I still found there is something else that drives students away. That is the fact that we have so many other wonderful things life has to the offer that seems so fun and enjoyable. When students find that something else that seems to be more fun and enjoyable such as attending that favorite amusement park or listening to music rather than learning the material, they tend to focus on the recreation activities than studying. Remember what I said earlier that avoidance leads to poor concentration.

I personally have spent time away from academia and joined an art association for two years where I learned how to draw and paint at a higher and detailed level. I use the techniques of multiple colors, drawings, and diagrams that relate to real-life interests students that they can relate to. Remember what I also said earlier in the previous chapters by getting to know your students and finding out what their common interests are. Using examples of their interest and linking that to their ability to learn can enhance the teaching process.

Use your imagination to make teaching enjoyable. Understanding similarities and differences between concepts will make students learn the material much better. As I said, pictures and drawings are effective tools when learning the material. You heard the saying a picture is worth over a thousand words.

Also, take the time to have students study tables of data. They do not have to memorize the data unless that is part of the teaching curriculum. Diagrams, pictures, and tables make excellent quiz and test questions. Having students look at other hidden backgrounds in pictures and diagrams can help students memorize and learn the material faster and can help answer different multiple-choice questions. Understand there is no single or correct way to teach and have students learn the material. You have to research what seems right, and you can do that through innovation and imagination by staying mentally, physically, and spiritually fit.

# Chapter 8

# Effective Presentations

Characteristics of great educators include the ability to develop appropriate relationships with their students. Building trusting relationships create an environment that is safe, positive, and a productive learning environment. Having a patient and caring personality is also a necessary factor. Being compassionate and being sensitive to student differences in learning is important. Educator dispositions correlate well with student's ability to learn, develop, and grow.

Knowing their learners is necessary too. You should be able to understand the cognitive, social, and emotional development of learners. Take time to understand how students learn at a given developmental level. See how learning progresses like learning progressions. Learners have needs and abilities where instruction should be tailored to the needs of their learners.

There should always be a dedication to teaching. Being passionate about the kind of work, you do which should always include student's success. Enjoying the subject area and always being dedicated to the work itself. An excellent educator should always help and give time.

Engage students in learning as a life long pursuit. Three main types of engagement include cognitive, emotional, and behavioral. The content needs to be interesting if the students are going to be interested.

Let us look at what effective educators do right in the classroom setting. Organization and clarity are necessary. Educators need to explain the content clearly, be well prepared, make difficult topics easy to understand, establish the context for the material, make the objectives and each class clear, make material understandable and memorable, and use examples, details, analogies, and metaphors to be interesting. The educator should seem to be dynamic and show enthusiasm, enjoy the subject matter and be self-confident. Instructor and individual student interaction should be perceived as fair especially in the methods of being evaluated should be seen by students as being approachable and a valuable source of advice, and even on matters not directly related to the course.

There should be a thorough command of the field, contrasts various theories, discuss viewpoints, shares them with the class, presents facts and concepts from related fields, and gives the student a sense of the field which includes past, present, and future directions and origin of ideas and concepts.

There should also be instructor and group interactions. This helps stimulate, direct, and paces interaction with the class. It also encourages independent thought and one should be able to accept constructive criticism. Be sure to use wit and humor effectively. Being a good public speaker as learned from Toastmasters International for Communication and Leadership has helped me with my ability to teach students. You should also be able to know whether the class is following the material and be sensitive to the student's motivation. You should always be concerned about the quality of teaching.

To carry out excellent teaching, the following points are what teachers do wrong in the classroom setting. If you decide to ask a question to the class and call on volunteers, you will probably only get a response from one to three people or you may even answer your own question. Most students in the classroom avoid eye contact. I also do not recommend calling on students' cold. If you decide to call on students without giving them time to think through the problems, then those who seem intimidated will not be following the lecture or hope you will not land on them. The minute you call on someone, other people feel calmer and breathe a sigh of relief.

I also find it dull just to turn PowerPoint slides one after another unless you carry out a mix of excellent presentation skills, which will be discussed later on in this book. It is also a mistake to fail to provide variety in instruction. Effective teaching consists of more than just PowerPoint slides, but it also consists of doing board work, storytelling, multimedia, activities, carrying out assignments, and doing bookwork. The more you put variety in your work, then the more interesting the class will be.

When students work in groups, remember all students need to be accountable in the learning process. Make the group work a learning environment that is cooperative. You want to promote the development of both cognitive and interpersonal skills. Another mistake I found from teachers who teach is failing to establish relevance. If you want to provide better motivation, it is always a good idea to begin the course by describing how the content should relate to important technological and social problems. Be sure to relate the student's experiences, interests, and career goals. Carry out this procedure when you introduce each new topic.

Do not give tests that are too long. If you want to evaluate the potential of your students to be successful professionals, then test their mastery on both their knowledge and skills you will be teaching and not their speed on solving problems. Another mistake I find educators carry out in their classrooms is they keep the course dull and teach the same content year after year. Take time to provide incentives and opportunities for improving courses.

It is also a mistake to teach without clear learning objectives. Make courses coherent and tests fair and write learning objectives and explicit statements of what students should be able to do. You will need to teach using objectives as a basis for designing lessons, assignments, and making exams. Above all, the biggest mistake that educators do in the teaching profession is to disrespect students. If you give students a sense that you disrespect them, then the class will turn out to be a rotten experience for everyone regardless of what you do.

What makes an effective teacher in the classroom setting includes expert communication skills, strong listening skills, strong knowledge, and passion for the the subject matter, friendliness and being approachable, caring relationships with students, strong work ethics, humor, ability to multitask, kindness, leadership, flexibility, calm demeanor, classroom management, and excellent preparation and organizational skills.

After mentioning these wonderful ideas, effective educators wonder what can be done to give powerful and better presentations. Exceptional presenters should take the time to open up in front of the classroom. Being organized and taking charge of the classroom is needed. You want to look poised and sound prepared. Powerful speakers take the time to persuade, influence, and entertain the audience. As educators, we can do the same thing. You want your teaching to be well structured and defined well enough to get your messages through.

Exceptional educators show enthusiasm. If they do not show and sound passionate about their work, then there is no reason why other people will not be passionate about their work. They also teach from the heart just as other exceptional presenters do. I have always found that it is worthwhile to be engaging in the interactions with the students to get them to learn. As mentioned in the earlier chapters, you want to build rapport quickly and involve the students in the learning process often. If you want the respect from your students, then you need to connect to them as well.

When teaching and giving presentations to your audience, you want to be natural. You want to appear natural as well as to be confident. The better you understand your students learning styles, the better you can teach them and have them learn as much as they can from you. You will have a better chance of connecting and engaging with your students, and they will feel more comfortable being around you, which will lead to more chances to work with them.

Those educators who practice their teaching ends up improving versus those who do not practice ends up getting poor results. Exceptional teaching needs to become second as this will not fail when you are under pressure teaching in front of your students or even speaking in front of an audience. You can start practicing in your normal daily conversations when you can form better habits and learn from mistakes within your trusted friends.

When I teach my students in the classroom setting, I want to feel like I own the room. Develop that open communication style and present confidence and maintain the best professional manner you can be even in the most challenging circumstances. Hold yourself accountable for the successes and failures for the teaching you carry out, but do not get discouraged. Delivering exceptional teaching will not guarantee that you will teach well every time, but you should never feel like you will lose your ability to teach because your teaching was less than exceptional.

Every time you teach in your classrooms, you are also considered a public speaker. You can see the two roles are about the same. I have seen educators who lack the ability to teach because they do not commit to improving their teaching, do not take the time to learn how to present the material, do not take the time to videotape and critique their presentations, do not seek feedback from experts, do not know how to develop proper habits, and do not know-how to practice.

Those who present effective presentations in their teaching careers build a reputation for excellence, know-how to present confidence to their superiors, peers, and subordinates, increase their potential to make more money, have more clients and students return to you, become more versatile, build credibility, secure lasting relationships, make strong impressions, increase your ability to influence others projects the image of an educator who leads, and excel at leading, inspiring, and motivating others to learn.

Attention and grab opening statements are critical to any presentation or teaching. Take the time to add that attention-grabbing opening statement. Ineffective opening statements will affect your presentations. You want to set that first few minutes with your message that your message is worth their undivided attention. You want to lay the foundation and not go into extensive detail. That is where you are going to present the information throughout the body of your teachings.

You do not have to start with the objective statement in the lessons. There are more creative ways to begin your presentation. Good effective opening statements can be a quote, a statistic, a question to the audience, a news item or periodical, a poem, a rhyme, humor, a story that relates to your teaching, or even having them write something down.

Let us look at the components of an effective presentation. Always begin with a purpose. Think of yourself in front of the students in the classroom. Your presentation of your teaching is about to begin. You are determined to teach that class for that day.

Have your students ask the question if they can remember one thing they have learned today, then what would it possibly be? If they can answer this question, then they have been thinking actively, and they have identified the most relevant portions of your presentation. Build your teaching presentations to a purpose and deliver that purpose to the students in your classroom setting just like an effective speaker.

If you tell your students what they are about to hear, then they are more likely to hear and learn it. The more you define your purpose, the easier it is to frame your messages. Defining your purpose for teaching for each new topic will keep the information relevant. You want your position of the subject matter your teaching to outline the expectations of what you want the students in the classroom to learn. I have seen educators stop teaching a certain topic assuming the students understand the material.

I take the time to call out and quiz students on the the material I am teaching to check their understandings.

Sometimes, this cannot always be done in large lecture rooms, but it is still worth a try to get your students focused in the learning process. The earlier you find out about your students learning of the material, then the better it is going to be for you to adjust your teaching.

You will find the results on quizzes and exams to be much higher than those who do not take the time, to effectively monitor the students learning the process. Once you get their results, check to see which concepts they are understanding and which concepts need to be taught again. This is like a call to action to help the students again who are having difficulty learning the material. Remember when you teach, you are going to teach them what you are going to teach them, then you are going to teach them, then you are going to teach them what you just taught them. In other words, you want to keep getting your message across until the students understanding of the material sinks in. When you are finished teaching them, take the time to end with a purpose.

What you say first and what you say last is what we remember the most. In the previous chapters, we talked about having students study in short periods with breaks in between instead of long hour study sessions. If I were to do an exercise with my students and tell them a string of random numbers, and then later ask them what the first and last numbers are, then they will more likely to tell me the correct answers. However, if I tell them what was the middle number, then most of them or more likely, none of the people in the classroom setting will tell me the correct number. We remember and retain more by remembering the first and last of anything.

We start our presentations by establishing a purpose, and we should then conclude our presentations with that same purpose. The purpose statements provide the framework for the teaching presentations and the more involvement and interaction you have with your students, then you will see greater and better results. Ending a class with questions and answers leaves room for a discussion of the relevant topics presented. It is up to you as the educator if you want to leave room for a final question to get students to think actively before the next class session.

At this point in your teaching career and if you did everything you learned so far in this book, then more likely you are passionate about what you teach. Exceptional educators radiate passion about what they teach. Nonverbal communication is also powerful. The nonverbal messages you project will override anything you teach. Both your words and nonverbal messages need to be congruent.

Posture is important when teaching and even speaking in front of a group. People start judging you the instant they establish eye contact. They need to be able to see you as a winner. Their judgments are based on your appearance, posture, movements, eye contact, and facial expressions. Above all, they are going to see how you carry yourself in front of them. Your posture and carriage are indicators of one's confidence and comfort level. Again, remember first impressions last. Think of posture as the first line of communication.

Stand tall and attentive in front of your audience. Move with a purpose and keep your head and eyes up. Be comfortable to make eye contact even if you do not know your students well. Your openness in front of your students in the classroom should reveal your enthusiasm and passion for the subject. Again, we talked about this earlier; make sure you smile in front of your students in your classroom. You want the tone of the presentation to be positive as you begin your presentations.

Some educators like to keep their easily relaxed, confident, and open. Nevertheless, that does not mean you cannot have other body posture positions. Great public speakers know a wide variety of ways to use body positions to get their messages across. The fig leaf position involves holding both hands all the way down in front of you. It shows how timid and inexperienced a person can be.

Having your hands in your pockets shows nonchalance, passiveness, and overconfidence or even having your hands behind your back in parade rest shows, you might be hiding something. Another body position shows having your hands on your hips, which makes a person come across challenging, and overbearing or even having your arms crossed shows, you are looking restrained. Different body positions can be used in teaching if it correlates to the topics you are teaching. It is an an effective way to present and teach information since most students learn and remember by being visual learners.

Let us look at effective seating positions when we sit in front of our students on the table. You want to project good body language and look engaged so that others would see you as interesting. As long as you are interested in what you are teaching, other people will see as being interested as well. Do be careful of the nonverbal messages your posture is projecting. You can sometimes lean even more forward, which adds energy to your delivery. It is best to keep most of your forearms and your hands on the table. Square up your shoulders to the person you are teaching and with whom you are making eye contact. This allows you and your students to invite each person into the presentation. This also helps keep your feet stable. Even squaring up your shoulders to large audiences in different parts of the room can make you interesting. You want to draw them into your presentation. Do this when you are teaching and presenting information behind the lectern.

Presenting and teaching behind the lectern can be a powerful way to deliver effective teaching. You want to make an effort to connect with your students. Keep both your head and eyes up when teaching. I like to make eye contact with all parts of the room. Do not read your lecture notes to your students. It is okay to have notes on your lectern, but you want to be prepared to talk about what you are teaching. Stand tall and be sure to gesture when giving presentations. Make sure you do not lean over the lectern, but it is still okay to rest your hands on the lectern, and as mentioned in our previous discussions to smile.

Having your hands pointed out in a claw position is a versatile gesture. It shows you are presenting or teaching important points. Using your fingers when representing numbers is another way to effectively present your message.

Horizontal and vertical movements with your arms and hands to show comparisons can also make your point across. When using verbs in your communication, make your arms and hands movement describe the verbs you are using. When giving out dates and using timelines show your hand pointed straight out to show, you are certain about the facts. Keeping your head up and eyes up to make, you look more fully engaged.

Making gestures should be second nature through lots of repetition. Practice gesturing in your casualconversations where the less time you have to think about them. It is not a good idea to think about your gestures when teaching or giving presentations. Keep your elbows away from your ribs and keep gestures below your shoulders and above your waist. Use your hands when you need to make your teaching more like a visual aid. Of course, make sure you use both hands when gesturing, and when you are done, gesturing put your hands back at the side. Gestures should not be the focus of teaching. Only use gestures to help your students learn the material and remember theimportant points you are teaching.

Let us move on now to your voice. Again, you need to sound interested for everyone else to be interested. Add energy, animation, and excitement to your teaching. The volume of your voice should be moderate; but if you are teaching or speaking and want to add dramatic effects you can also talk loud, talk soft, crescendo your voice, or decrescendo your voice to make your teaching more interesting. A wide range of voice tempos can make you look interesting but only if it corresponds to the appropriate topics you are teaching.

Exceptional educators can be just like exceptional public speakers to deliver their main points. The pause in between messages can be powerful to show you are making a new point. In other words, speak, pause, breathe, and then speak again. However, just make sure you do not always do this all the time when you teach. Videotaping your presentations and recording your voice can also help you review your presentations until you feel you are improving the delivery of your messages.

Avoid using unnecessary filler phrases such as "um," "uh", "you know," and any extraneous phrases in your teaching and speaking. Get right to the point in your message you are teaching. You will sound and talk a lot better than you realize. Make sure you are never condescending to your students. I know educators are experts in their fields, but picture yourself as if you were learning something brand new. No one likes to be talked down or feel small inside.

You need to teach and speak to the interest of your students by providing real-life examples, stories, or even anecdotes that they can relate to in their everyday life. We talked about eye contact with the audience, but we can also use gesturing using our eyes. Different facial expressions such as rolling your eyes or looking engaged convey messages to your audience. Remember most people are visual learners and what they see is more likely what they remember the most.

Sometimes teaching in large lecture halls makes it difficult to call on all the students. It might help by engaging in sections of the audience so no one feels left out. This is what I call being generous with everyone so no one feels left out. You are the focus of the room and everyone is listening to you teach the subject matter. It is not a good idea to talk to the marker board, floor, or PowerPoint presentation. Minimize your time making eye contact with these inanimate objects. I have noticed some educators make a seating chart to get to know the names of the students. That is up to you. If you feel it will get your students to be more engaged, then that is your decision.

Change the dynamics of the room by focusing the The majority of the time through your teaching presentations. It will help you make eye contact, speak from a position of authority and command, have people look up to you, be easily seen and heard, easier to move around, and helps us express ourselves more completely and gives us a chance to add humor to our presentations.

There is no way we can determine exactly what people are thinking such as their thoughts, moods, or what their interests are, but we can pick up clues about how an audience or how our students feel. Nodding heads up and down shows that their students understand the material. Having constant eye contact shows they are following you in your teaching or even leaning forward shows they are interested. When students are smiling or laughing in the class, you know they are enjoying the topics you are teaching. If they are raising their hands and asking questions, then you know they want to be involved. When they are taking notes, this shows they are eager to learn and remember what you are teaching.

The point is you want them to feel relaxed, communicate, and get them involved in the learning process. This will effectively help you monitor what they are learning. The best way to teach is to teach and speak naturally and connect with your students by demonstrating that you are genuine in caring for their business, issues, and concerns. Your voice, the content you are teaching and your physical delivery makes an important point when teaching or speaking to your students.

Professional in teaching involves reflection-in-action, problem-solving, self-assessment, commitment, ethics, roles and responsibilities, mentoring, values, and risk taking.

Educators also take the role of leadership and accept responsibility to increase the quality of daily interactions with other educators, students, and parents. They have the understanding to improve the culture of the school. Recognize that educators are leaders and their roles vary based on age. They also have a responsibility to be informed about the development of educational policies and research issues. Understanding global educational and professional issues make educators more of resources for those who seek help. Educators have a responsibility to shape the quality of the next generations by teaching, mentoring, supporting, and praising their students to lead for success.

Let us wrap up this discussion and talk about goals for success. The first goal is teaching students study skills. Some suggested affirmations include teaching your students to tell themselves that they enjoy studying and that they are enthusiastic and excited about studying. Be sure to have them plan their study work throughout the day and browse through their textbooks before studying them.

The second goal is teaching students to have strong reading skills. Have them state affirmations such as telling themselves that they love reading and that they read in large word-groups absorbing even the most difficult material presented. Have them ask questions before, during, and after reading and put their ideas together into text notes.

The third goal is to have continued to improve their note-taking skills. Have those state affirmations that they enjoy taking notes and enjoy learning new material and developing creative ideas. Have them enjoy using colored pens or pencils and have them draw pictures, illustrations, diagrams, and tables because they make great quiz and test questions.

The fourth goal is to continue to improve memory techniques. Stating affirmations such as that the students enjoying remembering information and that they retain the material with completeness convinces the brain over long term to believe it. Students can use more motor and contextual/spatial memory techniques in their studies. Developing rhymes and key words using acronyms can also help. We remember by sight, sound, and touch. Have them use these senses in their learning of the material.

The fifth goal is to increase the student's vocabulary. They can use affirmations such as they enjoy learning vocabulary and learning new words daily. Have them enjoy taking the time to use a dictionary and thesaurus. Some higher-level readings can also boost student's vocabulary such as The Wall Street Journal. Of course, they do not have to read every article, but they can find a few articles that they might find interesting. The Wall Street Journal newspaper is full of higher-level vocabulary words used in sentences, which can also boost students reading, writing, and speaking skills.

The sixth goal is to be a better test-taker. Affirmations can include stating they look forward to taking tests and enjoying the opportunities to show others, what they have learned. Stating they are also confident and relaxed during exam time can take away feelings of anxiety and pressure. Have students learn and study something new each day. Encourage them to ask plenty of questions in class, and have them show confidence and a feeling of over preparation for the quizzes and tests that they take.

The seventh goal includes using concentration. Have students tell themselves that they can concentrate with ease and they can block out distractions automatically. Have them convince themselves that they focus on the concentration on the tasks on hand and will complete it accurately. Some of the things that they can do both in and out of school are setting short-term goals, which later became completed long-term goals.

The eighth goal is to have better health. Have student's state affirmations such as they enjoy healthy foods daily and able to exercise when they need to during the week. Thinking positive thoughts such as being healthy, having energy, and living life to the fullest can add more years to your life. It is best to check with your physician what food groups you should eat.

The ninth goal is to teach students to enjoy learning. Have them look forward to attending the classes daily. They should be interested meeting new people and form satisfying relationships. They should have a positive attitude that they can be a success. The learning process needs to be enjoyable and congratulate or celebrate their accomplishments. They need to have confidence and believe in themselves to enjoy the learning process.

The tenth goal is to think positively. Positive thoughts teaching your class and wanting the best for your students is a noble deed. Being proud of your student's success and not being jealous of them will make you into one of the best educators out there. Know that smiling is powerful. It fights off depression and studies have shown you will live longer. Sometimes, it might be good to find the good about the bad things that happen in our life and learn from them. Realize that you as the educator make a huge positive impact in the lives of your students, which makes our communities stronger.

# Chapter 9

# Futuristic Teaching

Technologies and pedagogies are constantly changing the way educators teach, students learn, and the classroom environment itself. We wonder what the classroom will look like in the future and will our jobs and careers change. Do know that artificial intelligence and robots are not going to replace human educators any time soon. We are not there yet in that advanced technology era, but blended learning is on the rise.

Blended learning is an education program where students can learn through the delivery of its content and instruction through digital and online media. Algorithms will play a big role in the learning process. In other words, choosing which students sit together based on what they know and how well they know it. The algorithms will decide what problems the students should be working on and providing educators with the next lesson plan to teach.

These technological tools will combine with traditional education. This should allow the simultaneous diverse needs for each student. Instruction then becomes further personalized and learning models can be redesigned that integrates multiple instruction.

Interactive digital media decided on instruction and determining lessons for diverse students can take place by the use of algorithms.

We are hoping that the future of classroom design where technology allows furniture and the objects around them interact. Imagine learning about your favorite subjects in ideal places by having the walls of the classroom change its digital scenery or perhaps even interactive objects helping you along your studies. Video surveillance may also be a common thing in classrooms where educators can monitor the interactions of students. Perhaps turning some classrooms into work environments may be a lead to better transitioning from school to the work environment.

There will be technologies that will shape the classroom setting. Cloud computing, augmented reality, and three-dimensional printing are paving its way into the education system. Using Google Glass and other Augmented Reality-enabled wearable devices, student can explore the world even without holding up a device. Even virtual field trips are possible with augmented reality. It would be better and more interesting to learn about subject matters by being in ideal places.

Three-dimensional printing is already in the market. However, who is to say even more sophisticated printing will take place in the future. It will mainly benefit engineering students and teachers or professors. The point of these three-dimensional printers produces working minimodels so they can learn about engineering design principles. Using computer-aided design modeling software, three-dimensional printing allows students to experiment freely with the designs they are making without expending a lot of money and time.

There will be many other subjects that will require some forms of visualization. In effect, the cost of three dimensional printers will decrease which will allow more educators to be able to reconstruct complex models and teach theoretical concepts. Understanding molecular structures and configurations are not easy to grasp, but by printing out physical versions of the structures, this will help students understand the concepts better.

Cloud computing will continue to change many aspects of society mainly in the education setting. Students will need an electronic device to access their homework and other learning resources found in the Cloud. This means students will not have to bring their heavy textbooks to school. They will have constant access to their reading materials as long as they have an internet connection. This also gives students the freedom to work on projects or homework whenever they feel like it. The digital library will also be accessible when the campus library will not. Being sick may not be an excuse anymore once students have all of this digital access.

Cloud computing gives an online learning opportunity. It seeks to visualize the classroom. Schools can be able to set up cloud technology and setup online learning platforms for students to attend classes in a virtual environment. Cloud-based virtual learning environment allows students to access many kinds of learning content and participate in discussions. Assignments and tests can be given to the class, which will minimize the need for students to be present.

Educators will require another channel for interactions and discussions. The many interacting opportunities will allow more ideas to flow freely and be aligned with real-world scenarios where collaboration will be common. Social networking tools can be incorporated to help with collaboration and team building. Educators can lend some guidance based on the responses they receive.

This will be a great feedback tool, as it will allow a social-based approach to education.

Educational settings will become more digitized. Flexible displays may be lightweight, flexible, and thin. We may be able to roll them up into tubes or fold them just as if we do with paper and newspapers. Having plastic electronic paper will be durable, and students will not be able to tear these plastic electronic papers like regular paper. Another positive feature is there will be more information stored in these plastic electronic papers versus regular paper.

Biometrics has been associated with the security industry. It helps to identify fingerprints, facial recognition, and voice. When we look at this in terms of education, some schools are using it to prevent truancy and to borrow books from the school library. However, this feature can be more powerful for the educator by providing invaluable feedback and understand how students absorb and understand the learning content. Using this same form of analysis, biometric technology can be used to ascertain how effective the course is or to understand learning styles. Assessing information how students learn by getting details based on where they look during online learning sessions can be powerful. The data can then be integrated with interactive an adaptive learning system that adjusts the content to suit the students learning style. The eye movement patterns can also guide the delivery of the content, which takes, into account concepts students are having trouble by spending longer times in particular sections.

We have seen we have moved from using the blackboard and then to the whiteboard. The next type of board we might see in the future is a giant touchscreen LCD screen. These types of screens will allow a greater amount of interactivity. Having a screen attached to the computer will be capable of generating infinite combinations of images, sounds, and videos. These types of enhanced digital boards will be capable of detecting many touch inputs from many different types of students simultaneously.

Instead of using those common big boards in front of the classroom, it might be a giant tablet with an LCD screen sitting on top of a table. Students will be able to sit around the table tablet and be able to swipe on the board to move images around, or type notes with their onscreen keyboards. Students will be able to collaborate live with peers from around the world by manipulating virtual objects in realtime.

Motion-sensing technology can enable students to learn sign language and how to play a musical instrument by detecting their hand movements. This type of technology will be able to provide the necessary level of interaction for students to be more engaged with learning. Learning the game design process can also educate students. Having students learn basic game designing skills will help them develop broad skill sets such as learning language, storytelling, drawing, and even problem-solving. The point is having educators move away from the traditional classroom setting and letting students have fun and learn while they play games will help them as they grow up using this technology and having higher levels of excitement. Students will be able to see this appealing and captivating and they will want to continue to learn more.

Understand that schools will continue to evolve to satisfy human desire for better education. In today's competitive world, without excellent schooling, our nation cannot progress. This is seen in businesses that end up closing. Just about, all of the jobs are going to countries where both education and training are established. The biggest problem in education has it is now more expensive. Competitive schools are now adding infrastructure, which is making education expensive. Technology is going to skyrocket as technology progresses.

According to the Principle of Globalization, products and services will become affordable and evolve into the future at a faster pace. Schools are not any different. There is no need to globalize the school system from scratch. Many schools are already online which offer courses that do not require students to attend campus or even stay in student housing. Face-to-face discussions should be common once more people do so. I know because I have successfully tutored students on Skype and Video Gmail worldwide. Many people take online classes to enhance their career paths, enhance their knowledge, and look for promotions to higher positions and higher salaries.

There are excellent educators in most institutions and are not limited to one school. Students will have better opportunities to work with teachers or professors of their liking that are available online. This applies to students whether they are part-time or full-time. Excellent educators are hard to find in school settings during these changing times. Some students flock to popular classes, while other students barely attend any classes. Having classes online taught by the best educators, students around the globe will benefit more than an educator who does not care. Some students may decide to take online classes to supplement their regular courses for a fee.

Other students may take an online course if there regular educator at the school is not good enough to teach. This brings more revenue to popular online teachers or professors and even motivates them to teach better and better. Globalizing education means allowing students to take online classes at the schools they attend. This substantially increases the quality of education for students.

Online classes make availability and flexibility attending and learning the classes easier for students. In those traditional classrooms, students cannot go back to the earlier class periods or even fast forward to later class periods. Having more excellent educators reaching more students online is more effective in teaching where students have the option to learn during the day or during nighttime.

Making these online classes available in the education system can be affordable. Most schools depend on limited revenue from students and the government. Opening their doors to the global market allows more people to attend their online classes and the huge amount of revenue being made for excellent educators will make them continue to stay in the teaching profession. You will not even have to deal with disciplinary issues in the school system. Being an online teacher or professor can even be a high paying profession. Schools will still have to find innovative ways to have students carry out hands-on projects.

We have talked about virtual reality, which will be a great development soon. This age of automation shortly will revolutionize the education system. Devices that students can experience in virtual reality will make the classroom experience effective for online students and might make up for the hands-on the experience carried out in classroom settings.

This should not be a threat to those educators who fail to become excellent educators. Those who are interested in the education system but are not effective in their teaching ability can still help online educators by doing research and working for them. The market will grow and there will be more demand for research associates in the future.

Successful online educators will be looking for research groups to find updated information to deliver the best quality lectures and provide better interactive classrooms and laboratories. As technology keeps advancing at higher levels, future classrooms and laboratories will also be advanced. A lot of money from the government will make this possible. The best educators will constantly need to update their research and training to stay current in the global market. Research in preparing toprovide the best education online will grow as a global industry.

As schools provide great services to the world, their capability and revenue will also grow towards an evolutionary path. By globalizing education, schools increase the market size and will earn more revenue. This will bring the cost of education down, make global education a possibility, and provide more jobs and career paths for excellent educators. This will also help underdeveloped countries to grow as well.

Schools will compete to offer the best education possible out there. Future online schools will establish research departments to provide the greatest needs for their students. More students will learn faster by attending these online classes from around the world. Of course, there will be intense competition in this increasingly competitive world. Students will be looking for the best online classes, whereas schools will be looking for excellent educators out there. High technology and low-cost education is possible in the future.

We will also be helping underdeveloped countries to become modern. In this day and age, many villages do not have schools, and if they did have schools, most people cannot afford to send their children to school. Children are expected to earn money for the family, but in some countries, this might be illegal and catching those who commit crimes is not easy since the population is poor.

Education for children and families needing money is a starting point to initiate development for these countries. Having a paid-to-attend education system might be thebest hope for these countries. Even families could be paid for their children attending school. Private organizations may want to invest in these educational industries. In return for this investment, students can work for these organizations after graduation so the companies can get both interest and profit.

Education can be affordable even for private investment companies to invest in. Having paid education will result in dramatic improvements in those communities. It will also control crime and increase the morale and standard of living as well. The focus will change from daily survival to future advancement taking place. There will be a new future for them and many generations to come.

Of course, there will be risks, to begin with, but there will be better benefits along the way. Having a huge number of global employees and combine that with plenty of global jobs from an increasingly global economy, we will have a more productive world. Having this approach will transform these countries into advanced nations. Have your students when you teach them to think of education as an industry rather than as a luxury for only the privileged.

As technology gets better and better, I hope that students will be able to see learning not as a chore, but as a the pleasing part of their life, which involves their participation to always want to read more and learn new things. Effective educators will need to adapt to changing trends in technology as well as continue to keep current in their professional fields.

# Chapter 10

# Evaluations

The comments are given in this chapter reference the best experiences I had with my students at the University of California, Davis. I was a Calculus Grader for four years at the University of California, Riverside but I never received any comments from the students. Nevertheless, I still did an outstanding job grading many different levels of undergraduate math courses and the privilege to successfully work with many different university math professors. I leave the reader to read the comments below who I served greatly and have influenced tremendously and made a positive impact in the lives of many of the undergraduate students, I've held in General Chemistry and in Organic Chemistry.

# General Chemistry Evaluations

## Comment #1

Harmi,

I hope your vacation is going well! I was wondering if you knew my chemistry grades. I would like to find them out before I have to return to school. Please email me at my email address. Thank you for being a wonderful and caring T.A. for my first quarter at UC Davis.

## Comment #2

He really wants us to learn and is prepared to help us out during discussions & labs.

## Comment #3

Has the motivation to teach with pride and respect.

## **Comment #4**

He encourages us to do well in Chem. He helps us a lot in preparing for our exams.

## **Comment #5**

Always available for help. Tries to make sure everyone understands.

## Comment #6

Definitely enthusiastic & tries hard.

## Comment #7

Harmi, for his first year teaching, puts great amounts of time and energy into our learning of chemistry and I commend him for that.

## Comment #8

Tries to help as much as possible.


## Comment #9

He took the time to make us worksheets for review.

## Comment #10

Tries to help us succeed.

## Comment #11

Care for the students wants to help.

## Comment #12

He spends time on practice problems.


## Comment #13

He has taken a great interest in preparing us for the exams. He wants us to do well.

## Comment #14

He is very knowledgeable in chemistry. He understands chemistry very well. He can explain it.

## Comment #15

Taking time to make up problems that can be helpful to the students.

# Comment #16

Very enthusiastic about his work.

# Comment #17

He is always available to help students who need extra help, and takes the time to make worksheets.

## Comment #18

Harmi is always prepared. He knows what he is talking about. He is knowledgeable about chemistry.

## Comment #19

I think Harmi is excellent in TA. He knows chemistry and explains terms to the best of his knowledge. I feel prepared after attending his discussions and I know that Harmi will be there to help me out via email or via in person.

## Comment #20

Harmi encouraged us to do multiple homework problems, and he helped us in discussion section on them. He also gave us practice quizzes for the midterms, which were very helpful. Thanks!

## Comment #21

Harmi usually came prepared for class and had good intentions in getting our class to do well. He was available for office hours and was nice about helping and making his students understand.

## Comment #22

Predicting what to expect on midterms & finals. Giving more homework problems.

## Comment #23

Always willing to help students out with problems.

# **Comment #24**

Harmi understands the material and is excellent at answering questions and showing us how to solve difficult problems. The only aspect he needs to improve is going through the material and discussing what the professor has said in lecture. Overall is a good TA.

## Comment #25

He tries to help us the most he can, he offers to have additional study groups before midterms.

## Comment #26

Harmi definitely knows his stuff and is capable and responsible. He takes lab work very seriously.

## **Comment #27**

Keeping us on track on the homework. Giving advice on studying.

## **Comment #28**

Very dedicated to students. Encourages constantly doing homework.

# **Comment #29**

Well prepared. Nice Guy knows his stuff.

# **Comment #30**

Harmi always concentrated on mistakes that we might make at the beginning of each lab. He was very strict in upholding the rules.

## Comment #31

Helps us think independently, but should help us a little more.

## Comment #32

Makes us work on sheets to study.

## Comment #33

Take discussion section very seriously. Always have helpful review questions, which he passes out at every discussion.

## Comment #34

Gives worksheets for each chapter. The additional problems help with the midterms.

# Comment #35

Handouts.

# Comment #36

He has handouts with sample problems at each discussion.

# Comment #37

I appreciated the problems he brought to class. He was very well prepared.

## Comment #38

TA is well prepared & available to answer question.

## Comment #39

He responded well to students who showed strong effort for completing assignments, motivating us to do well and try harder.

## Comment #40

Helpful when asked.

# Comment #41

Harminder is an adequate TA (His best attribute is he speaks English).

# Comment #42

Good preparation & knowledge.

# Comment #43

Organized.

## Comment #44

During O. H. and after lab Harmi was very receptive to questions & very helpful. Those times were very helpful in my understanding.

## Comment #45

He was lay back & knowledgeable when he took things seriously.

## Comment #46

Nice Guy.

## Comment #47

He is Nice.

## Comment #48

Harmi is cool!

## Comment #49

Way he explained how lab was going to go.

## Comment #50

Very friendly, approachable, willing to assist students.

## Comment #51

Very prepared in lab prep.

## Comment #52

Don't be so shy!

# Comment #53

Instructor seems to be very knowledgeable but needs to not to be afraid to instruct. I feel the instructor worries too much about over teaching until it seems as if he holds back. Overall I think he is a nice person and wants to help other learn.

# Comment #54

I think Harmi is a fun TA. He always has a great attitude.

# Comment #55

Good attitude.

# Comment #56

Harmi tried his hardest to explain to us the lab. He responded to any email that I gave him and had high expectations for me, which made me do better.

# Comment #57

Forgiving, not uptight, easy to talk to.

# Organic Chemistry Evaluations

## Comment #58

Great attitude towards students.

## Comment #59

Explains things well. Good supplement to attending lecture.

## Comment #60

Shows good understanding of material explains things well. Very clear.

# Comment #61

I like the way that you teach. The only suggestion that I have is to tell students to come up to the board and solve problems in front of the class. Thanks for a good discussion.

# Comment #62

Harmi really tries to get us to think by encouraging all the students to participate in the discussion sections rather than just one or two.

## Comment #63

It was good that you asked the students if they had any questions, and that you paused to make sure students understood.

## Comment #64

Really knows the material well and is able to clearly explain/workout problem.

## Comment #65

Your explanations were a bit roundabout sometimes, so I think the students would benefit from a more direct approach. I liked how you always asked if anyone had questions and tried to draw people into the discussion by asking questions. We sometimes just need a little more time to think about the answer Even a few seconds more would be beneficial.

## Comment #66

Harmi is very willing to help. He does not make you feel you have asked a stupid question.

## Comment #67

Harmi was available for outside help. Good job for first time TA.

## Comment #68

He provided extra work to help us learn material better (for more practice).

## Comment #69

Very smart & informed. Knows his Ochem.

## Comment #70

Knows material well.

## Comment #71

Very patient answers our questions w/ clarity & encouragement.

# Comment #72

His knowledge of material.

# Comment #73

Knows his stuff.

# Comment #74

Knows material well.

# Comment #75

Knowledgeable of material.

# Comment #76

Very clear when he explained something.

# Comment #77

Harmi knows the material of the course very well.

# Comment #78

Harmi has a profound enthusiasm for the material andenthusiastically assess students. He did a good job.

# Comment #79

Knows work really well, confident, and capable.

# Comment #80

Good at explaining, seems to know what he's talking about.

# Comment #81

Knowledge of material very good.

# Comment #82

Very well prepared for discussion with examples, sample problems, explanation of assigned homework problems.

# Comment #83

Knowledge of material.

## Comment #84

He knows his stuff.

## Comment #85

Comes in prepared and ready to answer questions.

## Comment #86

Stays until all questions are answered; last one out the door.

## Comment #87

Harmi strength is that he attends to the needs of the students. He answers questions to where we are then able to comprehend the material better. He has a positive attitude towards his students and is a great T.A. -Recommended to others.

## Comment #88

He explains very clearly. I really enjoy attending this discussion section.

## Comment #89

Cover material very well.

## Comment #90

Harmi tried very hard to make sure we understood the information he presented to us. He presented much more information than necessary, adding info to fill in gaps & making it easier to grasp ideas.

# Comment #91

Harmi tries very hard but he lets himself go excessively fast on too much material. He has a lot of knowledge of the subject and is willing to help.

# Comment #92

Harmi explained things clearly at times and when we had a question, He would answer it right away. He also has a sense of humor that he uses at times to ease up the tension in the class.

## Comment #93

He knew what he was talking about.

## Comment #94

Depth of subject matter.

## Comment #95

Knows the subject matter ok. Has notes prepared for lecture and sometimes HW's answers. It was good he went over HW before turning it in.

## Comment #96

Harmi did all the homework assigned to us and was always ready to answer any questions.

# Comment #97

Tried to answer questions.

# Comment #98

Harmi goes above and beyond in his section preparations - thanks again Harmi for the practice midterms & for doing the homework last quarter!!

## Comment #99

He always prepares a good explanation of the lab at the beginning of class.

## Comment #100

He makes an extra effort w/practice exam to help us review and stimulates interest in chem beyond the lab.

## Comment #101

Harmi- great TA! He even makes practice tests for us + and love them because they show me what I need to study more of and my weakest point. Harmi is helpful and he shows an interest in our learning process.

## Comment #102

Gives additional info to help clarify… makes awesome practice exams!

# Comment #103

He knows his material well. Very friendly & helpful towards students.

# Comment #104

Gave practice exams - - helpful!

# Comment #105

He is a nice person, personable, grade.

## Comment #106

Practice tests and solutions helped immensely.

## Comment #107

Reviewed lab briefly before lab period.

## Comment #108

In the beginning, he had full explanations and spoke to us, very enthusiastic.

# Comment #109

Show interest in course material.

# Comment #110

He made up his own practice midterms, which were helpful.

# Comment #111

Harmi is an extremely nice person and very knowledgeable in chemistry and always willing to help. I think he should get more rest though, he always seemed so tired and overwhelmed.

After graduating from the University of California, Davis during the year of 2001, I was accepted into the Inland Empire Faculty Internship Program where I attended workshops throughout the year and carried out an internship at Mt. San Jacinto Menifee Valley Campus. I was allowed to teach at many community colleges. Being an Adjunct Chemistry Professor allowed me to work with a wide variety of students. I have included the best comments from different schools combined below. The majority of the students have gone on to rewarding careers, whereas some of them have got accepted to universities, programs of their choice, and even training academies, and even some students receiving scholarships for their entire undergraduate education. They were a great pleasure to work with and will be remembered.

## Comment #1

As classes went by his teaching became better.

## Comment #2

I understand more about chemistry, although there were better explanations than the ones given by this instructor. His knowledge of the subject matter is impressive.

## Comment #3

The instructor provided the class practice tests, but the practice test and actual test differ in some ways.

## Comment #4

I am truly surprised to not see "Dr." before his name. For he has profound knowledge.

## Comment #5

Excellent.

## Comment #6

I have never noticed him being tardy or leaving early.

## Comment #7

I have definitely expressed my opinions he definitely listened & gave help.

# Comment #8

Implies safety rules well.

# Comment #9

He always telling students to wear safety goggles at all times.

# Comment #10

He is excellent when it comes to safety it would be better if he demonstrated more of the labs.

## Comment #11

The best I have seen.

## Comment #12

He always make sure we r' wearing our goggles.

## Comment #13

I love chemistry it is exciting and enlightening course that will apply to my field.

# Comment #14

The course is interesting my favor favorite part is lab. I think if Prof. Gill would teach lecture I would have a better understanding.

# Comment #15

Mr. Gill is very organized and clear. He explains exactly what to do and walks through it with us.

# Comment #16

I wish Mr. Gill could have been my chem. professor instead of my lab partner.

## Comment #17

Taught well in class, material well presented just need to talk louder.

## Comment #18

He is very helpful and ensures everyone's safety by sticking to the rules.

## Comment #19

Mr. Gill is great I would take an other course with him. His teaching ability is outstanding he clarifies anything & is always ready to help.

## Comment #20

Class time is used very well. Instructor clearly lays out assignment and helps when needed. At times, he is long winded in answering simple questions; however, he displays his knowledge well.

## Comment #21

He is very nice and open. I always feel that I can ask you help "y I'm lost.

## Comment #22

He is very friendly, funny guy. I recommend him to anyone.

## Comment #23

Good instructor that knows his materials well very helpful and instructs materials well in lab.

## Comment #24

Mr. Harminder Gill, a little quick in explaining, but is ready to answer any concerns or problems faced using the lab. Gives a quick summary of what is expected during one hour of lab.

## Comment #25

Gill is an interesting instructor. Like I said earlier it seem like he knows what he is doing.

## Comment #26

Is smart but seems to feel rushed in explaining. Needs to explain more.

## Comment #27

Mr. Gill great.

## Comment #28

Mr. Gill as an instructor is great. He do his reaction to wooden pencil is somewhat disturbing or funny.

## Comment #29

He is ok, not great but all right.

## Comment #30

Presented material clearly + return tests promptly. Makes it comfortable to approach him w/ questions. Great teacher!

## Comment #31

Professor Gill provided a very structured and outlined class that was very rigid. He provided many study aids to help improve the learning experience of this course.

## Comment #32

Follow the class procedures and lecture materials in this class.

## Comment #33

He answers everyone's question thoroughly. He is respectful & helpful. He is firm & strict to his word.

## Comment #34

The slide presentations were very helpful.

## Comment #35

He has done a great job in presenting the subject matter in a short period although harder topics should be more discussed thoroughly.

## Comment #36

He promptly gives back assignments. He has a vast knowledge of the subject matter, and presents it well.

# Comment #37

PowerPoint, to have clear materials to read. Explaining well on the information.

# Comment #38

Teacher is knowledgeable in chemistry subject. Lab assignments and exams are returned promptly.

# Comment #39

He is well prepared with his slides for lecture; he really does make use of all the available class time. He tries to answer every question as clear as possible. He is very "by the book," nice but also strict.

# Comment #40

He has covered every chapter.

# Comment #41

Punctuality, safety, well explanation, fairness, thorough and knowledgeable. I could see that he is trying hard to teach students to know. He has a good temper.

## Comment #42

Returns assignments in a timely manner. Covers course material in line with outline.

## Comment #43

Professor Gill has made a great effort to make sure each student understands the material before continuing on to the next subject. In the 6 weeks, he has done a great job at constructing a lesson plan that is easy to understand.

## Comment #44

Gave our assignments back promptly explained definitions gave good examples that helped for our test.

## Comment #45

Presented PowerPoint well to correspond to textbook.

## Comment #46

The professor has done a good job in presentation. While he does not go into as much detail as I would like (me being a physicist). He does present concepts well, despite the confusedness of the other students.

## Comment #47

The notes through the PowerPoint slide show have been especially helpful. The notes were exceptionally comprehensive.

## Comment #48

Teach by the syllabus.

## Comment #49

The material was organized. We were given a course syllabus & we never fell behind. He worked at a good pace. He had a good understanding of the course material. Which made the material easy to understand. The course was taught well. The tests were fair & we knew what to expect.

# Comment #50

Answering questions and stayed to end of class to do that. I am usually the last one in lab.

# Comment #51

Instructor used both PowerPoint slides and board work effectively. Students were engaged. He asked questions during the lecture which the students answered. The students also asked questions when something was not clear. He spoke clearly and at an appropriate pace, He gave students a chance to write things down and ask questions before moving on.

I decided to start working with several different tutoring companies throughout the nation and even started doing private tutoring with many different clients in different communities. I ended up having just as much success tutoring my clients than I had being a teaching assistant and a professor. As time went on, I even had the privilege to tutor students worldwide on Skype and Video Gmail. These places include California, Utah, Washington, Ohio, Pennsylvania, Colorado, New York, Florida, Texas, Minnesota, North Carolina, and in England. Many students have reached their goals being accepted to universities and programs of their choices. Feel free to read the comments below.

# **Comment #1**

Professor H is a great tutor; he has helped my son on 2 occasions to prepare for an important honors algebra II test. I wish I had started the tutorial sessions sooner in the semester. He is very clear in the explanation of the subject and working with my son to bring him up to speed for the tests and for overall algebra knowledge. He also has been very kind about our last minute requests for help prior to a test. I would recommend him to parents with the highest rating for his availability and clear direction that he gives during his tutoring. It is apparent watching him work that he has a comprehensive background working with students at different levels of knowledge and study. Currently 5.0/5.0 Stars.

# Comment #2

Prof H. is very professional, organized, caring, and communicates well, giving feedback to parents. At this time, it is too early to tell regarding the actual success of the tutoring. Highly recommend based on experience so far. Currently 5.0/5.0 Stars.

# Comment #3

Pretty good. Professor H. knows his stuff. I just wish he could have helped me with the Statistics Program: JMP. Currently 4.0/5.0 Stars

## Comment #4

Great tutor! There when I needed him even on short notice. Highly recommended! Currently 5.0/5.0 Stars.

## Comment #5

Mr. Gill is a great tutor. He was always available for me whenever I needed him and really helped me get through a tough class with patience and understanding. If you need a chemistry or a trigonometry tutor, why not get the best? Go with Mr. Gill! You will not be disappointed. Currently 5.0/5.0 Stars.

# Comment #6

Currently 4.0/5.0 Stars.

# Comment #7

Schools on Wheels sent me an email. I have sent them a very favorable response. I recommended you to a couple of people. How far away do you go to tutor? Is it only in the Riverside area or do you go as far away as say Montclair? Thanks.

# **Comment #8**

Wanted to let you know we are very pleased with Jacob's PSAT results. With your help, he went from a 170 as a sophomore to 192 as a junior. Most notably, his CR score jumped from 45 to 62 and his Math and Writing slightly improved from 65 to 68 and 60 to 62, respectively. I appreciate you focusing on CR where he had the most room for improvement, thank you!

# Comment #9

Hi Professor H, I appreciate your quick call back regarding tutoring today. Also, what type of payment (cash,check) do you prefer for tutoring? See you tomorrow. Thanks.

# Comment #10

Hello Professor H., I haven't finished them yet, I will attempt to get them finished by today. I'm just trying to get as much done of the assignments for the exam that I can(: But, thank you! Did you have any availability for tomorrow by chance? Thank you for your time.

# **Comment #11**

Thank you all for your prayers and support! I passed, and will be starting the RN program June 22!

# **Comment #12**

No, I passed the class that is it for me. I have graduated from my bachelor's program. Now I am just waiting to see if I am accepted to USC for their film program. No, I did not. Instead, I will be attending Cal State San Bernardino for National Cyber Security in January.

# **Comment #13**

Thank you for the update on Gavin, and thank you so much for working with him, he is learning so much from you. I wish we had found you sooner! I do not think I can leave a review that will do Harminder justice. I have had tutors for my kids in the past, but none of them is even in the same league as Harminder Gill. He helped my oldest son (19) prepare for the Military ASVAB for the Air Force, and taught him more in a few months than he learned in high school. My youngest son (14) struggled with Math and was averaging 60% on tests and quizzes; he is now scoring consistently over 90% and has even had a couple perfect tests. Aside from his ability work with kids, Harminder is always on time and prepared professional and an all-around very pleasant person. I would recommend his services to anyone who asks. I am very thankful we found him.

# **Comment #14**

Good Morning Harminder, I want to thank you for everything you have done for Gavin, he could not have gotten this far without you. I would like you to continue with Haydn, if Friday is the only day you have we will continue with that day. If another day during the week comes available I would rather have another day Monday-Thursday if possible. Otherwise, we will keep Fridays. Thank you.

# Comment #15

Hi professor Gill, I just wanted to follow up with you and let you know that I got my ACT results and I actually did better than I thought, I got the score I needed to be accepted into the finance program at my school! I want to thank you anyway for taking the time to send me the practice tests and all!

# **Comment #16**

Hi Harminder! My test went well! I got a A! I'm studying in a group for graph theory test! Hi Harminder! Everything went well! I got A in stats and differential equations, but a C+ in graph theory class! Happy holidays!

# **Comment #17**

Dear Professor Gill, The two-hour session for physics helped a lot on my physics midterm, although I do not have the results yet. I feel like I got an A. Finals are coming up next week with Multivar on Thursday at noon and Physics on Friday afternoon. For Multivariable Calculus I am allowed a one-page sheet where I can write notes and formulas for all the chapters covered. Would you be available for a two or three hour session on Tuesday the 8th to prepare for Math and the same on Wednesday the 9th to prepare for Physics? Thank You.

# **Comment #18**

Hi Harminder, It is so nice to hear from you. Nina is doing very well and has submitted her college applications to both several Cal States and UC's. We are anxiously waiting to hear where she gets accepted and what her final choice will be. She is extremely busy, as you can imagine, but getting all of her work done and excited for her upcoming graduation. Thank you for the message. Happy Holidays!

# Comment #19

Got it back today. Received a 74% (C) which is the highest grade I received on any Calculus test the last 2 years. Thank you for your help I do not believe I would have gotten a grade as high as this one without you.

# Comment #20

I would have to double check with her, but I believe she ended up with a B on both test and in class Thank you very much for your help and checking in on her.

## Comment #21

Hi, I did well. I finished the class. Thank you for asking.

## Comment #22

Good evening, this is a great recommendation. We greatly appreciate your help can you please sign it and seal it in an envelope. Please bring to tutoring we have to include it with the whole package. Thank you.

# Comment #23

Peace, Love, and Gratitude At this time of the year, we are so grateful for the many friends like you who give support and encouragement to the thousands of children in Southern California who are without a home. Thank you most of all for the hope you give to our homeless students that they too can have a chance for success through education. On behalf of all of us at School on Wheels, may the peace, love, and joy of this holiday season strengthen our children, our families, and our communities? With gratitude.

# **Comment #24**

Hi Harmi - 8AM - 1:30AM is a very long day! I know you got a lot done, and I hope it all went real well, but be careful that you do not burn yourself out by putting in such long days too often. Your ability to teach so many different courses is truly amazing! Your students are certainly blessed to have you as their tutor. Thank you very much for such a comforting and consoling letter. I will treasure it forever.

## Comment #25

Praise God! He is intervening for you! You have a lot to offer, and God is gifting and preparing you! Never give up and always seek His wisdom!

## Comment #26

Very nice! You are a good teacher!

# Comment #27

You are a very classy and knowledgeable young man and we will miss you... thank you from all of us...

# Comment #28

Professor, Katie responded that she is on track and no longer requires tutoring.

# Comment #29

Hi Gill, I wish you lived closer to Murrieta! I have an Algebra 2 student and I'm having a very tough time finding a good math tutor for her. I will definitely let you know when I have a student to run by you. Hope to talk soon.

# Comment #30

Thank you, Harminder! Mom called about 15 min ago and said her daughter found a classmate? That can help all weekend. You are the best. Thanks for trying to help me. out!

## Comment #31

Harminder: Your e-mail sounded like you feel like many people do. Many of us in society feel like outsiders, like we don't always fit. You will learn to find you place your niche and thrive. As our territory grows, there will be a place for a special young man like you. Blessings.

## Comment #32

Thank you much! You were a big help however I do not think I am going to take the exam! I actually switched majors and now I do not have to take chemistry and I will still graduate on time! Thank you again though.

# Comment #33

Good morning, Thank you so very much for not only providing us with the attachments, but for taking the time to do so and provide the material. We appreciate you are reaching out to do this on your own time. Please do not forget to let me know when you are available. We are available on next Friday evening, around 8 p.m. We will not be available on Saturday and Sunday. Again, thank you!

## Comment #34

Kharissa scored a C on her test. That is great. She had a low score before the teacher let her re-take the ones she missed! The teacher is so proud of the enormous change in her grade in such a little time. Thank You MUCH!

## Comment #35

Just wanted to thank you for your time. I appreciate it. I got a B in the class. Thank you for all the help.

## Comment #36

Thanks Harminder, I am feeling much better. Thanks for thinking of me. I know the song.

## Comment #37

Thank you so much for thinking of me Harminder. You are very kind. I hope you have a lovely weekend and stay warm and dry in the rain. Hope to see you again soon.

# Comment #38

Hello wonderful Volunteers, as we close 2015, I would like to sincerely thank every one of you for your dedication and selfless commitment. You are truly the heart of the OI and I have loved being part of such a wonderful team. In the first week of January, I will be leaving Ocean Institute. It has been a pleasure to serve as Volunteer and Public Programs Manager this past year.

# Comment #39

Thank you for catching that. Moreover, thank you for sticking with Riverside Citizen Science.

# Comment #40

Good Afternoon Harminder, Fantastic! We are looking forward to your presence and contributions on Saturday.

# Comment #41

You are sweet, thanks. Hope to see you again.

# **Comment #42**

Dear Mr. Gill. Thank you so much for your kind email. It was a pleasure to speak at the Care Giver Symposium, and your email made it even nicer! I have heard of Toastmasters, and appreciate the information! Thank you so much for your comments! Have a fantastic day! From My Heart to Yours,

# Comment #43

Hi Harminder, I am probably going to let my family into Disneyland on Labor Day weekend and then head back to the Burbank area. I will keep you posted on the next trip where I plan to stay for the day. I am glad TM has helped you to meet people. I am glad we met. Big Smiles.

# Comment #44

Dear Mr. Gill, Thank you for your email. It would be great if we could meet from 10:00 am – 12:00 pm on Tuesday, Dec 10. I am reviewing calculus notes and will send over a list of some of my problem areas tomorrow. I have a paper due this week so I am trying to finish that too. Thank you again for meeting me on Tuesday.

# Comment #45

Thank you, Harminder. Your condolences are greatly appreciated.

# Comment #46

Dear Mr. Gill, Chemistry went great! I got an 81% on the final and it bumped me up to an overall C+. So I passed. I appreciate your assistance the weeks prior to the test, they definitely made a difference.

# Comment #47

Hi Harminder, I have written down all the problems I need help with. I've been trying to work practice problems, I've had a busy week with exams in chemistry and genetics. Yes, this Thursday at 9am-11am. Thank you for all of your help. Blessings.

# Comment #48

Hello Harminder, I'm sorry it took so long for me to reply but my final grade was just posted this week and I did make an A in the class. I hope things are going well for you!


# Comment #49

Dear Harminder I appreciate your response. Please keep us in mind for the future. Thank you.

# Comment #50

Yes I did I feel more confident :) Hi I am doing well I now attend Grambling State University in Louisiana and my major is biology. I love it thanks for helping me study and prepare for the SAT.

# Comment #51

Harminder, Thank you for letting me know that you will no longer be volunteering at our library. Suzanne and I appreciate the time you contributed as a Computer Lab Volunteer. I wish you the best of luck with future endeavors.

## Comment #52

I got a 93.5/100.

## Comment #53

I will definitely do that. Thank you so much Harminder! God bless you.

## Comment #54

Oh so sweet! Do not give up! You are a good person! Hope to see you at the candling service!

## Comment #55

Thank you, Harminder! I will pass on the link to our adult non-fiction buyer. Very impressive web site.

## Comment #56

Thank you for the ecard. That was so nice.

## Comment #57

Wow, that is awesome! Great job!

# Comment #58

Harminder. We have been missing you. If you are still busy on Tuesday evenings, please at least come join us on Saturday receptions like tonight! Our friend.

# Comment #59

Happy Holidays to you too Harminder!! I hope you have a wonderful time. In addition, hopefully get a little break from work. Nutritionally yours.

# **Comment #60**

Hello Harminder, I am pleased to hear you are interested in volunteering at Orange Terrace. We would like to have you come in and assist us with shelving. You may contact me at your earliest convenience so we can schedule you for an orientation and have you get started as soon as possible. Thank you.

# **Comment #61**

I will be notifying Olga that you have PASSED the classroom portion of the mediation training. (There is no grade assigned in this class.) She will be in contact with you after all the exams are in about the next step--the observations and co-mediations. Good luck. It was a pleasure to work with you again.

# Comment #62

Happy Holidays to you too Harminder!! I hope you have a wonderful time. In addition, hopefully get a little break from work. Nutritionally yours.

# Comment #63

Great advice and much appreciated. I am still in the learning mode. The video clip advice is valuable and I will upload in my downtime in March. Thanks again and I will pursue the information in Toastmasters. Hope you enjoyed your b-day. Take care.

# **Comment #64**

Hi Harminder, That is great. Congratulations! I hope your book ends up in the hands of many, many people. And I can definitely pass along your website. Keep up the good work!

# **Comment #65**

Hello Harminder! For some reason, I always remember you! You always worked so hard to become a better speaker, and I liked it when you played your instrument at the Christmas party, remember? Sorry to hear you are not in Toastmasters. I am actively pursuing my Accredited Speaker (that's different from a Qualified Speaker). And I still remember you had an idea for glasses(?) or some type of new technology. Glad you are still researching. Let's keep in touch!

# **Comment #66**

`Hello Harminder, Thank you so much for your reach out of congratulations! Yes, I ended up deciding I'd try my hand at an Area Governorship this year. It's been an interesting process so far. I will most certainly have new perspectives once this journey is complete.

# Comment #67

Thank you Harminder. It was nice meeting you today. You take care too ~ Thank you for the beautiful card.


# Comment #68

Hey Mr. Gill, Just letting you know that I not am tutoring this weekend. The midterm feels like it went well. Please let me know that you received this email. I look forward to hearing from you soon.

# Comment #69

Hey, Mr. Gill I will not need tutoring this Saturday. Just thought I would also let you know that I got an A on the midterm. I hope you have a good weekend.

# Comment #70

Good Evening Mr. Gill, I just thought I would let you know that I received an A on my final and an A for the overall stats class. Thank you for all your help. I wanted to let you know as soon as they put up the grades. Thank you.

# Comment #71

Good to hear from you Harminder. Lemon St Toastmasters had a banner this year when we made DCP and with 17 members. For now, I am on vacation for 6 months in Thailand with a return in May 2016. Congratulations on your DTM.

# Comment #72

Thank you Harminder, Our Club is doing well. Happy Holidays to you.

## Comment #73

I got it! Thanks Harmi. I have skimmed through it & absolutely love how you have made so easy to understand. I will be using it to help my boys with their understanding of chemistry. Seems like you have been busy. That is great. Take care.

## Comment #74

Thanks, Harminder. Best wishes to you.

## Comment #75

Congrats on publishing a book!

## Comment #76

Hey Harminder! Happy Birthday! Hope you had fun day in your excursions in Southern California! In addition, enjoyed the cake you about yourself :) Blessings.

## Comment #77

Happy Valentine's Day Your Friend

## Comment #78

Thank you so much for the update, Harminder. I will follow up as well and see if we can get things moving! Please let me know if you do hear back and are able to schedule a session. Thanks!

# Comment #79

Thank you so much for your interest. You are truly an asset to Kimberly Crest. Happy Easter We are very pleased on how you and the other docents of the 2016 class have embraced Kimberly Crest. Looking forward to hearing from you.

# Comment #80

Thank you so much for thinking of me Harminder. You are very kind. I hope you have a lovely weekend and stay warm and dry in the rain. Hope to see you again soon.

## Comment #81

Good morning, Harminder! I certainly hope I get the pleasure of treating you again. You have a great day yourself!

## Comment #82

Hi Harminder, Thanks for thinking of me. My friend has this and I've learned to be careful! Thanks. Be Well. Blessings,

# **Comment #83**

Hi Harminder, Found this in my spam just now. It was a pleasure talking with you too. You can email me with specific requests of my interesting life as a Jail RN for San Bernardino County Sheriff's Dept Milwaukee Sheriff's Dept. Pittsburgh [Allegheny Jail] I recall you mentioned you're interested in research. Or any Kimberly Crest stories we discussed.

## Comment #84

Harminder Thanks much on 2 counts. I appreciate your sending each of the pictures you took. There are a couple that are great and might be used in a future quest.

## Comment #85

Thanks too for helping give a tour. You are so energetic and have learned a lot of information well. You are part of a dynamic docent class. Keep up the good work, leave quiet time in each room so folks take it all in, and enjoy. Best. Thanks again.

# Comment #86

Dear Harminder, I am very sorry to hear about that. Thank you for helping me with both chemistry and math, you have helped me so much. I hope everything is well.

# Comment #87

Thank you Harminder!! I appreciate your message. I will see you soon.

# Comment #88

Thank you Harminder.

# **Comment #89**

It was wonderful meeting you. I will have to check out your website. Perhaps you would like to address our Manuscripts later this year. We have had authors, screenwriters, people adept at putting novels & eBooks together, literary agents, cartoonists, software designers in computer gaming, historical romance authors, and many others. My talk on Monday will be equally unique as we have never had anyone just talk about storytelling. They will probably think its OK, at least this once, as I am their new president and I think they would like to know more about me. If I am doing it right, you'll find our latest newsletter attached. Looking forward to conversing with you again. Hugs,

## Comment #90

Thank you very much! I'm sure this chart with help. I will reach back to you once I secure a specific time with Aliyah regarding future sessions.


## Comment #91

It was a pleasure speaking with you today. Nancy and I look forward to meeting you at Starbucks, 1575 E. Ontario Ave, Corona, CA 92881.

# Comment #92

If you are on Facebook, you may want to check out our group East vale Garden Group. The members are knowledge rich; someone will be able to answer a question. Hope you are well!

# Comment #93

It was nice meeting you too! I have attached the pic I took of you. Have a wonderful day, (Talk Show Host/Producer)

## Comment #94

Good morning Harminder, How thoughtful of you. Thank-you!

## Comment #95

I wanted to let you know Mehran made the Commander position. He just wanted to invite you to the Pass in Review/Change in Command ceremony this Friday. He does not know exact time yet but can text you tomorrow.

# Comment #96

We were on your first tour Sunday at the beautiful Kimberly Crest house. William is the tall person with the Ph.D. in polymer chemistry and I am the shorter person with the M.M. in piano performance. Thank you for the nice tour. It was our first time there and I hope to come back often. Because I am a pianist, I was going to ask you about your clarinet playing but I saw that you needed to get to your next group. We also had to meet our realtor to look at a few houses. We have been looking there for a while because we are thinking of moving there from Palm Desert. I hope that you and yours are well. Thanks again,

# Comment #97

Hello professor Gill Here is my syllabus for this 8 weeks summer chemistry class have a great weekend, thank you so much for all your assistance with my goal of earning desirable grade. I will see you on Friday June 10th at 1:00 pm CT.

# Comment #98

Hi Harminder, thank you. Yes, you can post my photo on your website. Take Care,

# Comment #99

Thank you so very much connecting and for your input. I found your insights invaluable and truly adding to the experience. I also am excited about reading your book. Keep me posted!

# Comment #100

He passed, thank you! We are getting ready to move and Isaac will be a "senior" at Sky view HS in ID. Yay! Take care and thanks again.

# Comment #101

I want to thank you for all of your help with understanding chemistry. Thank You,

# Comment #102

The drawing is so fun! How did you do that? Do you have some kind of program? I am so impressed,

# Comment #103

Awesome Harminder! Let me know how it goes. I will be in on Monday. Have a great weekend! Thanks,

# Comment #104

Hi Harminder! Thanks so much for getting in touch, I appreciate the advice! I wish I could have stayed longer, but I have a deadline that I had to meet last night, and I was getting a bit crunched for time. If you have notes to share, I would be beyond appreciative!! :) I think you are a great contact that could help promote our app! As I mentioned to you yesterday, it's totally free so it's pretty easy to share with parents. Hopefully, I'll hear back soon! :)

# Comment #105

Thanks so much for all the information! I will not share the links. I will also try to make one of Joel's speaking engagements in the future. I caught a bit go what he does on video from David T. Fagan and it was good.

# Comment #106

Hello Harminder, It was wonderful meeting you this week! Please remember you have a much bigger presence than you think you do!! Have a wonderful weekend!

# Comment #107

It was a pleasure meeting you as well Harminder, and I will keep you in mind if I hear of anybody who is looking for a tutor. I'm so glad to hear you got a lot out of Debbie's event and wish you tremendous success with your business!

# Comment #108

So great to have met you! Let me know how I can help!

# Comment #109

Thank you for the info Harminder! I hope you are doing well!


# Comment #110

Thank you for the great information! I had to work all day Saturday and Sunday so it was unfortunate that I hadto miss all of the great speakers on those two days. Huge congratulations to you on such a major accomplishment! I wish you much success and hope Hollywood comes knocking on your door! All the best,

## Comment #111

Hey Gill, I love your website! I read thru the whole thing. What a great book. The chemistry of cosmetics sounds sooooo interesting! Especially for me as I make my own all-natural beauty products. Wahoo Namaste!

## Comment #112

Dear Harminder It is good to read back from you and to know that you are doing well and fine. Yes, I hope that I could get job but for now, I am yet to get one. but if you do not mind to help me, then it is fine. Warmest hugs and regards.

# Comment #113

THANKS HARMINDER ~~!

# Comment #114

Thank you so much Harminder! I really appreciate you taking the time to help us to improve Grade Potential!! I have sent you a link in a separate email that you can click and confirm your review. Best,

# Comment #115

Hello Harminder, Thank you for reaching out and wishing my trip well. It did in fact go easily and gracefully. I hope your journey wherever you were located went just as well.

# Comment #116

I am happy to hear from you and was planning to tune in with you tomorrow. Now is even better. I am wondering what you may want my help with regarding my particular expertise. It would be my honor to assist you in anyway. I remember you spoke about your particular for this and also your desire to connect more easily with women. Let me know if I missed anything or if you'd like to add something to this list and I would forward to hearing from you soon. Warm Regards,

# Comment #117

Harminder, That could very well be ME in the near future. I can see you are a VERY good networker. Great follow-up & commitment to connecting people! We are of like minds. Cheers,

# Comment #118

Hi Harminder, Awesome! Then yes I will be happy to count that as both required shifts. The Pilgrim training will be at 11 am - 12 pm. You will have lunch from 12 - 12:30 then jump in the afternoon shift at 12:30. Thank You,

# Comment #119

Dear Harminder When I count my blessings on Thanksgiving, I will count you twice! Best Wishes,

# Comment #120

Thanks for thinking of Harminder. The seminar was terrific. We had a good group of people. What a nice idea a girl cave! Best.

# Comment #121

Harminder you are such an amazing man! Thank you :) I hope you have an amazing weekend and know that we appreciate the hard work you do for us!

# Comment #122

I got this email professor Gill. Thank you so much.

# Comment #123

Hello Harminder It is nice to hear from you. Things have improved for me. There is no comparison between now and one year ago. I have other things going on that are keeping me occupied. It sounds like you are staying busy so that is good. Go do something fun and enjoy yourself.

## Comment #124

Dear Harminder I am always glad of you too and thanks for your message. I love you too very much and I believe in my feelings towards you. Yes I send my deep kisses and hugs to you my love. I really appreciate you and thanks for your concern.


## Comment #125

Hello Professor Gill This is Jerry from Illinois. My final grade from chemistry is B. I wanted A but I am happy with B. Thank you so much for all your help Professor Gill.

# Comment #126

Hello Harminder, I'd like to thank you for being so kind. Upon meeting you, you set a tone of kindness not many people do, that's much appreciated! What got you started in being a tutor? I know it takes a lot of patience and you must be very skilled in your expertise of study to break down a subject as difficult as "Chemistry" and make it simple for others to understand. As Einstein says "Genius is taking the complex and breaking it down to it's simplest understanding." I will be sending you some information on my education company but just wanted to touch bases with you to Thank You Harminder. Have a Nice evening and talk to you soon.

# Comment #127

Hello Harminder! A pleasure speaking with you today. Again, make sure to please be in touch with me if there is any other offers that you are considering so I can go over upgrading options or help you with future orders. Have a great day! With thanks.

# Comment #128

I am grateful that you are getting signing better and learning quickly. Please see attach worksheet 1-12. Please let me know if you have any question. See you next week! ASL Instructor.

# **Comment #129**

I am writing in regards to Harminder Gill. He has tutored my oldest son in. He was extremely kind, punctual, and knowledgeable. He would come to our house at our convenience. He would take time for our son and made sure he was prepared for his tests. He would even go the extra mile and call to follow up and see how he did on his assignments. If you are ever in need of a tutor for your child, I highly recommend Harminder Gill. Thank you for everything Harminder. Have a blessed day!!

# **Comment #130**

Yes, it is a small world! I thank you for the kind offer of availability, I appreciate it very much. No worries on the pricing of your book. If you do not mind, I will purchase from you directly, but will have to do so after this coming Friday (payday). I would love to do lunch and catch up, let me know what works for you. Friday or later works for me. Well Harminder, I have to get back to it! Thank you for your reply; I look forward to meeting with you soon. Thank you.

# **Comment #131**

Hello Mr Gill; I'm so happy to hear from you, I have been trying to get in touch with you, Rosie did a great job, but as you know she is in her 1st year of high school and she need help in math, initially I was hoping to locate you to ask if you can help me with my 7 year old she had a hard time last year and she still needs a lot of help with reading. I was wondering if you have the time to tutor both of them and how much is your fee. Thank you for keeping us in mind I really appreciated, hope to hear form you soon.

# Comment #132

Dear Professor Harminder So here is a basic idea of what I have been learning in class that I struggle with: *Chapter 1 is about fundamentals. So I hope this helped you to see what I struggle with and thank you for your time.

# Comment #133

Harminder: you are the best!

# Comment #134

Harminder, Always great to hear from you. I trust that your tutoring will enable the gentleman to reach his goals. I hope all is going well for you. Take good care,

# Comment #135

Awwwwwwwwwwwwwwa! How very Kind of You! I have got a Terrible Head Cold & I am headed for Bed~ Hope all is well by you! Hugs. Blessings,

# Comment #136

I got some medicine so I'm starting to feel better. Thanks for asking Needed a 220 to pass! Thank you Harminder for all your help! (National Series Exam for K-12 teachers) Yep, all good! On my way to becoming a K-6 teacher! I'm on track to do my student teacher this Fall since all my testing is done with! Then I can apply for my credentials. Thanks for all your help!

# Comment #137

Greetings Harminder, Thanks for doing this research for us.

# Comment #138

Hi Harminder, CONGRATULATIONS on your new book. It sounds very interesting.

# Comment #139

Harminder, Thank you for your thoughts. This was indeed tough since it has also been less than a year since my passed. I was sorry to have missed the Brunch. I am sure it was a lot of fun.

## Comment #140

Thank you for taking the time to complete a survey regarding your recent visit to our Subway location on Limonite Ave. We are happy to see you had a positive experience. If there is anything else we can do do to make every visit a 10, please let us know. Have a great day! Thank You.

## Comment #141

Hi Harminder, Thank you for your email. I will definitely reach out to you if I think of anything else that can add to your cosmetic research.

## Comment #142

Mr. Gill, Thank you for taking your time to deliver my package. I arrived late last night to find also this package which is from you. Thank you so much.

## Comment #143

Dear Harminder, Thank you for this update on your career- you are doing some wonderful things. I heard that the Living Promise event was amazing; I'm glad you were able to attend. I will be happy to pass along this information to our alumni office. I have signed you up for the November 19 CNAS events and look forward to seeing you at the event.

# Comment #144

Mr. Gill, I have received your application. The next step will be training. You will receive an email with the training schedule and locations by the end of the month. Take Care, "Tax Volunteer Coordinator"

# Comment #145

Hi Harminder, it's Sonya from GP Tutoring. I just called about your student Dallas A. His mom called and canceled services. They really liked you and thanked you for your work you did with Dallas.

# Comment #146

Perfect! Thank you so much! Thank you! oh! did you get your gift? good! Thank you so so so much for all of your help.

# Comment #147

Thank you Harminder! I did well on the GRE. A bit above average, but I wanted to do a little better. Maybe I'll take it again! Thanks again for your help!

# Comment #148

TGreat start with Chris. His school funding begins mid-January.

# Comment #149

Harminder Gill! Hello, friend, how are you? I just bought the eBook!! I'm very excited to read it. What a beautiful website you made for the book. What hosting service do you use ?? I am in the market. :0) Happy holidays to you,

# Comment #150

Dear Harminder, when I count my blessings on Thanksgiving I will count you twice! (Ocean Institute)

# Comment #151

Harminder, I've just received my scores, and while my verbal reasoning and analytical writing stayed the same (which I wanted because I was happy with those scores), my quantitative reasoning score increased from 158/170 to 161/170, which takes me from the 70th percentile to the 79th. While I would always prefer an even higher score (like a perfect one), I believe this is a realistic and notable improvement and I am glad that I had you there to guide me. Thank you once again for all of your help.

# **Comment #152**

    Dear Professor Gill I wanted to let you know Mehran has an A- in AP Calculus all thanks to you. It was a challenging class for him and I am happy to see him face the challenge. Thank you so much. He did work hard to manage along with all his many other leadership duties as school Commander and CA Cadet Corps Commander. You have been with him a while and I can definitely see the improvement. You are without a doubt a very smart but also very humble and patient with him. You always show up before scheduled time so you can set up the boards in time for class, you are calm and you genuinely care for your students. Integrity and care are hallmarks of your teaching style. We appreciate you and look forward to last months of his high school years with you. Thank you,

# Comment #153

Happy Holidays Harminder it's Nikki!! Wherever you are celebrating, I hope you have a safe and joyous holiday filled with tons of laughter, fun, and sweet memories.

# Comment #154

I just wanted to take a moment to tell you how grateful I am that we are in each other's world and hopefully we will have the app.

# Comment #155

Awe thank you so much Harminder for writing back. I totally understand and so appreciate you taking the time to reply to my message, it means a lot.. Let us explore what the New Year brings, in the meantime. I will definitely check out your website and thanks again for reaching out. I wish you much success.

# Comment #156

I enjoyed reading what you have been up to since we last talked. You are certainly a remarkable man...even more so than was my impression when we first met. Your achievements have been numerous showing your creativity, excellent writing skill, and eloquence. I read the introductions synopsis of your books on each site. How amazing! Kind regards,

# **Comment #157**

Hi Harminder Thanks for coming to the Archives yesterday and volunteering. It was a pleasure meeting and working with you. The Archives are open most Mondays and Thursdays from 11 am to 5 pm. We are looking forward to seeing you again. OERM Archives.

# Comment #158

Thanks for your sweet note. I've always thought of you as a friend as well. I do hope you just watch MSNBC News once a day, to keep up on the world you live in. Take Care.

# Comment #159

Thanks for staying in touch, Prof. Gill. James is doing better in school. His teachers are now re-focused on his education after I hired an attorney to attend his IEP meetings. I think James needs to experience some successes to provide him motivation, which he lacked before. I hope that this trend will continue.

## Comment #160

You're a fantastic tutor! Chris truly enjoys working with you!

## Comment #161

Wonderful. You are doing a great job and making a difference in the life of others. That is what we are put on this earth to do. I am so happy for you Harminder

## Comment #162

Congratulations Harminder! I am very proud of you. I hope all is going well!

## Comment #163

Hi, you are a good man Harminder; do not allow people to Hurt You. Know who you are and let life happen. Everything works out in the end. Blessings,

## Comment #164

Love the kindness to the elderly man! Sounds like you are one of few making the world a better place!

## Comment #165

Hi, Yeah it's going okay so I decided not to continue the tutoring. I am sorry the people at Grade Potential said they would tell you! Thank you so much for your help!!

## Comment #166

Beautiful act of kindness Thank you for sharing

# **Comment #167**

You have a humble heart! That is always good because the Bible says God resists the proud. We all have to guard against pride and arrogance--it can so easily slip in, because it causes all kinds of pain in the end. Happy you involve yourself in so many activities. Though sometimes painful as you have expressed, they bring wisdom and insight to social situations and people in general. You are not wasting your time on meaningless endeavors, (drugs, and alcohol) and in the end, your life will benefit!

## Comment #168

I loved the story you shared with me about what happened at Starbucks. I am going to share it with my office!

## Comment #169

Thanks Harminder! It was nice to chat with you, too. Thanks for the nice words. I will check out your websites, and keep up all the great work!

## Comment #170

So glad to meet you. Thank you for the links.

# Comment #171

Dear Harminder, What sheer delight to have the chance to visit with you today. How regrettable it seems our visits with you are so infrequent. God willing, we can meet occasionally at a library for the pleasure of your good company. Meanwhile, we have yet to view a DVD, which we just checked out, "Genius," by Stephen Hawking, a 2-disc review of his experiments with volunteers to think like the geniuses of the past to answer today's toughest questions. With love and prayers.

# Comment #172

Keep your heads up. You are doing fine!

# Comment #173

Dear Harminder, I am pleased to say that I have completed the differential équations course and received a B in the class. thank you for all the help. Sincerely,

## Comment #174

You are an amazing tutor. Please don't let someone make you second guess yourself. Unfortunately, as you know, we just can't make every single client happy.

## Comment #175

Harminder, I will pass the information on. Thank you for letting me know.

# Comment #176

Hi, That's very sweet of you, however, I don't think it's necessary. Steve, the man I live with, has his Doctorate in Health & Fitness, and he keeps me up-dated on herbs &stuff. Very Sweet of you. I hope all is Happy & Well by you.

# Comment #177

That is wonder! What a great service you're doing!

# Comment #178

Hello Harminder! Great! Please do reach out and I am looking forward to hearing from you!

# Comment #179

Harminder: Are you still tutoring? I saw a friend who may be looking for someone. If so, please send me your current info so I can forward it to her. Thanks.

# Comment #180

Thanks for responding, Harminder.

## Comment #181

Good Morning Mr.Gill, My name is Nicole, I believe you spoke with my grandmother about the tutoring appointment later today. I am looking forward to meeting you and getting help with geometry, we will see you at 7. Thank-you.

## Comment #182

Congratulations! You do a lot of great work. Best wishes,

## Comment #183

Hi Harminder, Great start with Nicole.

## Comment #184

Good for you! Volunteering your services is rewarding for all.

## Comment #185

Thank you for your prompt response

## Comment #186

Congrats to you! One has to admire your desire for community involvement!

# Comment #187

Hi Harrmi - This is another big achievement. I know you will rapidly become their best docent and they will be very happy to have you! I agree that your emails are very helpful - and I also think that anyone that takes at offense at any of your suggestions is probably ignoring helpful advice.

# Comment #188

Good to hear you are doing well. Blessings,

# Comment #189

Sounds good! I will text you when we are close to arriving at LACMA. Have a great rest of the week and see you on Saturday.

# Comment #190

Hello wonderful Volunteers, As we close 2015, I would like to sincerely thank each and every one of you for your dedication and selfless commitment. You are truly the heart of the OI and I have loved being part of such a wonderful team. In the first week of January I will be leaving Ocean Institute. It has been a pleasure to serve as Volunteer and Public Programs Manager this past year.

# Comment #191

Thank you for coming to the Summer Teacher Workshop. It is my hope that you enjoyed your time with us.

# Comment #192

I appreciate your offer of group tutoring. The students in my program might be interested in it as a supplement to the one-on-one tutoring, which seems to be a major selling point with them. In addition, their schedules vary in terms of when they are available. ILS is having a workshop in Beaumont on April 22 and another in Upland on April 29. Would you be referring to these? I plan to attend both.

# Comment #193

Hi, We have assigned you to the Gonzales/Loza Garden at 649 Los Altos Dr. from 1 pm to 4 pm Saturday, April 22. Please arrive at 12:45 pm for your assignment. Please respond to this email so we know you received it. Thank you so much for volunteering. If this is not a convenient time or you have questions, please respond to this message. Thank you,

# **Comment #194**

Hello, I just wanted to say thank you for your note! It was very nice to read and we sure understand working within a limited budget. Thank you for the support that you currently provide the Ocean Institute and thank you for visiting us so often. The place is great to learn. Perhaps you will consider volunteering, sometimes that is the best way to learn about a position opening up here. Thanks again for your note and I hope you are having a wonderful and happy holiday season. With warmest regards,

# Comment #195

Hello Harminder, I read Nextscienceman 2100 and look forward to a sequel. You a very busy man! I am glad you will be attending the conference. I hope it will be worthwhile. Thanks,


# Comment #196

Harminder, Thank you! Have a great week.

# **Comment #197**

Hey, it is really a pleasure to hear from you. It looks like things are going well for you and that makes me very happy. Where are you working? I am keeping busy during my retirement so far and miss teaching. I taught part time for the first two years of retirement and that was great but then the principal changed and he did not like hiring retirement teachers so I was out. This year I had three different part time offers to teach but the time of day kept me from doing that since it would have taken away from my other pursuits. Keep in touch please. I play handball on a regular basis and see many former students there, some of them go back to the 70, and 80" s. Amazing Thanks.

# Comment #198

Mr. Gill, thank you for contacting the library about volunteering your time. The City's volunteer process is a bit lengthy as each applicant must be Live Scanned, interviewed, and trained. Unfortunately, we are into early December already and since the procedures can take some time to complete, I strongly doubt that you would be on board by month's end. In addition, all library volunteers are required to give us 30 hours minimum. There is quite a bit of training involved and we like to keep our volunteers for as long as possible since we invest quite a bit in them. If you are still interested in volunteering, please visit the City's web site (www.riversideca.gov) and listed under Human Resources is a link to Volunteer Opportunities. Thank you for your interest!

# Comment #199

Mr. Harminder Thank you for the contact. John was definitely a challenge. He is a great kid….I am really happy when students from High School go on to become a professional much less one in Chemistry so definite kudos to you. Have a great day…and yes, I am still here 28 years later!

# Comment #200

What a lovely, heartwarming treat to hear from you, Dear Harminder. Happy entire beautiful holiday season to you. Please join us at the next big get-together, after LACE. Loving best wishes to you.

# Comment #201

Dear Mr. Gill, Thank you for your email. It would be great if we could meet from 10:00 am – 12:00 pm on Tuesday, Dec 10. I am reviewing calculus notes and will send over a list of some of my problem areas tomorrow. I have a paper due this week so I am trying to finish that too. Thank you again for meeting me on Tuesday.

# Comment #202

Tell about copper pot that would have put on the stove with water and bluing ( a bleach or whites), and sheets boiled before being washed.. Show washing machine explained how used. Explain laundry tubs and rinse method. Dryer line outside among trees when weather good, inside when bad. Clothes pins from craft store only now. Pie safe for cooling baked goods.. Be sure to recommend gift shop or take them there at end of tour. Hope this helps, let me know if I can help any more.

# Comment #203

Harminder, We are very interested in discussing the tutoring position with you. Our son is currently in Algebra 2 with Trigonometry (more on the Trigonometry right now) and is hoping to be taking Calculus next year. He is also taking Honors Chemistry and he could use a little help in both. He is doing well in both classes but could be doing better and we would be looking to get him some help and review prior to finals so that he can do his best to finish out the year. If he does well he will be taking Calculus next year and we would be looking at doing some tutoring over the summer as well, to get him a little head start so that the beginning of the school year is a little easier for him. We are located in Rancho Cucamonga and would prefer to have sessions at our house if possible. He is fairly busy with school and baseball so we may have to accommodate your schedule and his. Please email back or give me a call if you think you can help and to discuss the details. Thank you.

## Comment #204

Fantastic job with Nicole! If her computer is old, she may need to email less attachments at a time. I hope they continue with you so Nicole can truly learn. Thank you!

## Comment #205

Dear Harminder, It's a short drive home for me, but I just got home after attending a private Mastermind dinner with Nancy. I hope to see you again this weekend. Congratulations on showing up today, whatever else happens. In the meantime, I'm attaching my Speaker Sheet, which I completed under Nancy's program. Good Night.

# Comment #206

Hey Harminder! Here's the website, sorry I just needed to head out there early! Hope you have a great day! With Great Love.

# Comment #207

Hi! Nice meeting you at the seminar! Yes, you did answer my question about the ingredients in sunscreen. Looks like you are up to some great things… I will check it out more. Wishing you the best!

# Comment #208

Hi Harminder, I spoke with Donna. They are very pleased with your help. Nicole is a good student but struggles in Geometry. The goal is to help her pass the course. Donna is on a limited budget, but wants to add a 3rd day a week until school is out. Keep doing your best!!!

# Comment #209

Thank you, Harminder! I continue to send support and luck your way!

# Comment #210

Hi Harminder, I'm so happy to also met you. I'll let you know soon as my website is working. Hope to see you soon. Bless ya,

# Comment #211

Hello Harminder, Monday from 3-7 works out pefectly. I have talked to Joe about your skill set, and let him know that we need to put you on payroll as soon as possible. It's not a whole lot of money, but it should cover your travel expenses. I will will have a more exact answer for you by the end of the week, as I do not want to over- or under-promise. Thank you,

# Comment #212

I know it...trust me I have talked to over 30 math tutors about this one; no one will touch it anything helps! Please let me pay you for some prep time for this one, especially if you are heading to the library for books.

# Comment #213

I am so glad to have met you. Most Scientist is forgettable. You are sooooo unique, charismatic, and unforgettable.

# Comment #214

Got it. I am sure your tutoring is helping Vanessa gain Confidence. Thank You!

# Comment #215

Hi Harminder, It has been awe inspiring and so humbling to read all of your emails and shares about how life-changing Fearless Speaker Emergence has been for so many of you! What I've witnessed unfold and emerge from you during and after the event has lit me up with joy! And if you remember...On day 1 of FSE, my goal was to get you to the level of courage (200) and all I can say is that you went WAY past that! So today...I just wanted to honor you for your courage, vulnerability, humanity, spirit, strength, and most of all, your willingness to take a stand for you and your speaker dream!! You ARE the voice, the creator, the stand for your own speaker path. Thank you for trusting me in being your guide to the ledge. Now... You can "build your bridge as you cross it" and get to the other side of your dream. I'll be cheering for you and believing in you ... every ... single ... step. Speak your dream,

## Comment #216

Excellent job! Vanessa only has 3.25 hours left of funds. I will check with Elia to see when they can access additional funds for Vanessa.

## Comment #217

Hello Harminder, Thank you for your great attitude about education. At this time, we can pay you to come in for four hours per week. Any extra time would be considered volunteer time. Can I ask you to switch your Monday, 3-7 shift to Monday from 5-7 and Tuesday from 6-8? If not, that should be okay. Thank you,

# Comment #218

Thank you very much for working with Nick. I am sorry he was a little strange about skyping and using his camera. I have changed your rate to $25 for this student, apologies on that mistake! I will email accounting and let them know to add an hour of prep time to your next deposit. Moving forward, I suppose you would need to tell me how much time each week you would need for prep. I can then run that by my boss and see if we are going to pay you for it directly, or if we need to talk to Nick about you logging it through his account.

# Comment #219

Congrats, that is a sizeable tip. You must have worked hard for them. Best Wishes,

# Comment #220

Hi Harmi - This is wonderful to hear -Congratulations! He must have been really happy with all of your great teaching and help. Wouldn't it be wonderful if all of your students would do this - it would make a great alternate source of income! But, unhappily, most students are struggling to make ends meet, so they are lucky to have enough money to pay for each of their tutoring sessions. Again - CONGRATULATIONS!

# Comment #221

Hi Harmi - I think this is great! You would have been a great mathematician - but you are very talented in many areas and could have received a PhD in almost all of them. But I think it is important to choose your favorite topic, and then specialize in it, and I think you did this when you chose to specialize in Chemistry. The only trouble (in my opinion) with this area is that it is prohibitively expensive to equip your own lab - and it is difficult to do research when you don't have such a lab. In any case, I know you will enjoy the books you have checked out - there are many very different branches of Math., and they are all interesting and useful.bridge as you cross it" and get to the other side of your dream. I'll be cheering for you and believing in you…every…single...step. Speak your dream,

# Comment #222

Hi Harminder, Thanks for asking! My feeling is that it went very well on Saturday, and the feedback I got from audience members bore that out. I was able to connect well with audience-much more so than in my other Keynote Concerts. This was my 3rd. Coming fresh after FSE was a HUGE positive, as I remembered and implemented more of Tiamo's suggestions, like pausing to let things sink in. I was much more comfortable being myself. There were a few much unplanned moments that some people told me were their favorites. As an unexpected bonus, the videographer I hired went way beyond the bare minimum we had agreed on of one camera. He had 2 cameras, and also recorded the sound separately through a lavalier (sp?) mic. I will be looking at the video today. Overall, I am over the moon! Thanks,

# Comment #223

Harminder, If you're still interested, I have some more books (law & politics) you are welcome to take away, along with some empty and blank binders/notebooks. Let me know what times suit your schedule and we'll make arrangements. I can be free any day/time except this Friday morning. Take care.

# Comment #224

Thank you for your diligent patience.

## Comment #225

With the latest bunch, it is pronouncing sounds in English that are not found in Korean: L, R, and F.

## Comment #226

I have let accounting know that we owe you $10 to make up the difference on the 2 hours you worked with Nick. Also, I spoke with Nick and you can go ahead and log 1 hour prep time for each session you work with him. Thank you Harminder!

# Comment #227

Wow! 10 extra hours from Mehran is quite a gift. Obviously, that family is very happy with your help! I will let you know as soon as I have a student near you in In Em. I wish I could fly you all over LA and OC! Those areas are busier for me this week.

# Comment #228

Greetings Harminder, It was a pleasure speaking with you as well. I look forward to reviewing your information. Thank you & Have a Blessed Day.

## Comment #229

It is okay Harminder. I sent Sean a recap of the emails you sent to me last week. We will let him investigate the rest. Thank you for your gracious heart in wanting to help Vanessa.

## Comment #230

Alex got an A on his math final exam and got an A in the class. Thanks for your help!

# Comment #231

Thanks for the information, Harminder!

# Comment #232

Hi Harminder! Thought you would like a picture from the Home Tour! Hope you are enjoying your Memorial Day weekend. Best,

# Comment #233

Very handsome! Thank you for sending! Keep me posted on the Heritage House and how it goes!

## Comment #234

Thank you, nice photos…hey, you look good in the Oval Office !!!!

## Comment #235

Hi Mr. Gill how are you, I'm blessed thank you for checking up, your a blessing to have as a tutor! I got an 83.33 on it. I was disappointed because I wanted the A. Although My final is coming up and I will get an A on that. I got a problem on my trig test wrong because I said it was a cos graph instead of sin, because it started at zero. I will not make that mistake again. God bless,

# Comment #236

I had a meeting with the house captains today and Nancy Sturmer had wonderful things to say about you Harminder! She said you were so enthusiastic. So your enjoyment of the event did not go unnoticed! Thank you again.

# Comment #237

Hello Harminder, It was so nice to meet you last night at the PBS SoCal (KOCE) pledge night. Hope you enjoyed yourself and the handmade wooden chair you received made by Alan. Look forward to hearing from you receiving the photo when you get your phone working again.

# Comment #238

Our chemistry teacher, Harminder (who is FANTASTIC), also wanted to know what he was working on exactly so he can bring in some materials. But if you / he doesn't know it's no big deal.

# Comment #239

Hi Harminder, Thank you for all the suggestions. Appreciate your taking the time to send. Good l luck with your phone repairs.

## Comment #240

Hi Harminder, great job with Chris. Enjoy!

## Comment #241

Woo hoo disregard previous email re mailing it. I got it now!!!

## Comment #242

Hi Harminder, Thank you for the information! It was a pleasure to meet you, as well.

# **Comment #243**

Good morning! You have no idea how much I appreciate you! I know a big part of this business is not only accommodating a student's academic needs, but also their personalities. On top of this, they are usually already pretty stressed out by the time they call us for a tutor. I think it happens often that a student would really like their tutor to do a lot of their homework. We are going to pay you no matter how much work you do for a student. If they feel comfortable with that, then it's their decision that they have to live with. Students are very fortunate to have you!

# Comment #244

Hey Mr. Gill, I did pretty well. I passed the class with with an A. Thanks for asking!

# Comment #245

I talked to her the other day and she'd said as much. You're the MAN, Harminder! Thank you for all that you do!

# Comment #246

Will be good to see you Harminder. We don't serve wine or alcohol, only healthy drinks and food. ;)

# Comment #247

Hi Harminder, Thanks for attending the workshops! I really appreciated your left-brained perspectives on things. I'll have to check out your work and forward it to my husband, who's a sci fi fan. I do enjoy sci fi, too, so I'll definitely check them out. And I'll keep you in mind if students ever need remote tutoring - what a great idea!

# Comment #248

Hello Harminder, Thank you so much for your interest in serving our homeless students. Let me know if you have specific questions I can help you with regarding online tutoring. Thank you. Lisette: Thank you for connecting us!

# Comment #249

Hi Harminder! Glad you found the place! Nice seeing you. Hope to see you at the next event in a month.

## Comment #250

Hello Harminder, Thank you for the message! I hope to discuss Victorian ideas worth you some day. In the least, I will ask Jo if I can be scheduled on the same days as you because I think it would be fun to discuss how to give better tours! Your colleague,


## Comment #251

Thank you for your contact information. My son, Troy Spieler, should be contacting you soon. Thank you,

# Comment #252

Hello, I'm glad you enjoyed the Ice Cream Social. Thank you for the name, I will forward it to Lynn. I am so glad you were able to attend the graduate luncheon. The gift shop contributed most of the gifts, I always appreciate their participation and generosity.

# Comment #253

Thank you, Harminder. Hope you have a nice one as well.

# Comment #254

Doing a Great Job/Very Professional.

# Comment #255

Very Professional/Great At Explaining Concepts.

# Comment #256

Dad Said That It Is Going Really Well.

# Comment #257

Sessions Are Going Excellent!

# Comment #258

Jordyn Said His Style Was Different But She Did Get A "B" On Her Test. Last Test She Got A "D."

# Comment #259

Harminder Is Great And He Wants To Continue To Work With Him.

# Comment #260

Skype Engagement. Tutor says it is A Great Fit!

# Comment #261

Hi, I just wanted to let you know I got an A on my chemistry quiz today. Thank you for your help, I will be sure to contact you the next time I need a session.

# Comment #262

Keep up the good work and welcome again to the lyft family.

# Comment #263

Hi Harminder, good to know! I happened to speak to Nikki last night, Goke's mom, they are really, happy with you working with Goke. Mom had her doubts of this working out on skyping, but she is super happy with the outcome so far! Thanks for all your efforts! Goke is supposed to mention he wants to bump up to 2 hours per week.

# Comment #264

It was a pleasure meeting you this afternoon at the Ted Wells lecture Harminder. I look forward to working with you as a docent at the Webber House and helping to further develop its docent and touring programs for the city of Riverside's historical, architectural, and cultural awareness. Hope to talk soon.

# Comment #265

Harminder, Thank you for reaching out so quickly. Any help you are willing to share would be most surely accepted. Much Thanks,

# Comment #266

Next Monday. I am working on my own to see if I can catch on and so far, I got a 25 (avg) on the sciences on practice tests! I will let you know if I need more help. Thank you for everything.

# Comment #267

Hello Harminder. I just wanted to thank you for spending time with me today. I look forward to future conversations. Good Night.

# **Comment #268**

Thank you Gill for sending samples of how to write a resume. I am so very grateful for my time is really running out. I will sit down today and work through as many as I can to my liking as a teacher and taxes for right now. I look forward to receiving letter of recommendation from you. I have a lot to accomplish within the time left. even though I am in Florida I will still keep in touch until I return in January. Thanks Again.

# Comment #269

Thanks sir! We are glad to have an epitome of knowledge as you influence knowledge in him. Thanks for all you do!!


# Comment #270

Hi this is the woman you asked earlier if I was interested in home schooling. My sister might be interested so if you want before you leave stop by next door. She would like some info about it. Thanks Knock on doorbell does not work.

# Comment #271

Good Morning Yes, I have added it to your account. Thank you and please let us know if you need anything moving forward. Have a wonderful week!

# Comment #272

Thank you Mr. Gill for you help, if anything my confidence in science is much better.

# Comment #273

Yes I got accepted into Mississippi Valley State University. My major is Engineering Technology with a concentration in Computer Aided Drafting Design and I have a 3.8 average. And i appreciate the tutoring.

# Comment #274

Good morning! I can't thank you enough! I was going to have to tell this family I couldn't help them. You are so wonderful!

# Comment #275

Hi Harminder I did well B. Thank you for asking.

# Comment #276

Comment #266 Hi, I did well on that quiz and I passed the class with a B. Thank you for your help.

# Comment #277

Just got hired this morning. Thank you Gill. I start to work tomorrow. It was about 35 of us in the class. Men and Women. I am sure I will do just fine.

# Comment #278

I received my scores from the last SAT and I raised my math score from a 530 to a 640.

# **Comment #279**

Hi Harminder, I am going through your student records and impeccable writing for one, thank you I can totally read it. I have attached a picture of the certificates area and you do not need to fill this out unless you are issuing one a COC or SL, So on a 3rd lesson you would write the COC# where the DL400 goes, same when issuing a SL you would enter it in the OL800 spot. If you are not issuing anything then leave it blank. Also if you can, staple or paperclip the SL with the forms and the students records so I can have it all together. Other than that they look really good. Thank you & have a fantastic afternoon!

# Comment #280

Hello Mr. Gill, It was a pleasure talking to you over the phone. Thanks for providing your email and welcome to BookBlast PRO! Below is a rundown on what we talked about.

# Comment #281

That is sweet of you. It may not be very soon but I will keep in touch for sure.

# Comment #282

You are welcome. I noticed you updated the subject line. It is nice to know that you give importance to these kinds of details. You have a fun-filled weekend, Mr. Gill.

# Comment #283

Good to hear from you.

# Comment #284

Thank you so much! Prayer means so much!!! It works! Have a great week!

# Comment #285

Thanks. Yes, things are going well. I hope the same got you.

# **Comment #286**

Wow Harminder! I'm exhausted just reading of your diverse interests. It takes a lot of discipline and perseverance to accomplish what you have. I really admire your ambition and proactive approach at achieving your dreams. I write also and it takes time and patience. Most of my works are religious poetry and short stories. I ordered 2 copies of your first novel, one as a gift. God bless,

# Comment #287

Hello Mr. Gill, Take care always! It was really nice of you to check what that missed call was about. Sorry if it seemed urgent. Have a happy weekend!

# Comment #288

The HR Block training is very good. You should do well.

# Comment #289

That's great! Wishing you the best of luck and lots of sales!

## Comment #290

Dear Harminder: Congratulations on your achievement(s). Thanks for keeping me updated on your activities!

## Comment #291

Excellent! Will do! Cheers to you!

## Comment #292

Thanks Harminder. I hope you are well. Will you be volunteering again this year? Be Well,

# Comment #293

Hi Harminder, Congratulations! That is fantastic. Big Smiles,


# Comment #294

Hi Harmi - What a wonderful compliment. Even if he/she never tells you what a great instructor you are, you can be sure he/she knows you are (just because they travel so long to learn from ;you). Congratulations!

# Comment #295

Thank you very much my friend.

# Comment #296

That looks really great! I will make sure to make a purchase!

# Comment #297

Great stuff, Harminder! We'll post about it! Thanks for sharing!

## Comment #298

Congratulations Harminder! Very cool!

## Comment #299

Hi Harminder, Brian said they will still work but read up on the manual to get better familiar with these cars. I will order you more Business cards and send the temp ones for now until your order comes in. Thank you Harminder for always trying to better yourself for your students. I love it!!!

# Comment #300

Hi Harmi - Thank you for this email - it looks like a great book, and I am very proud of you!

Best regards,

# Comment #301

Thanks for letting me know about it. Will Check it Out.

# Comment #302

Cool! Thank you!

# Comment #303

Nice! Keep a positive attitude, always! We can all become cynical if we let ourselves!

# Comment #304

Hi Harmi - It is good that she realizes how dedicated, conscientious, and expert you are. I hope all your future colleagues will take the time to realize this - it is clear that at least some of your former ones did not do so. Keep up your great work and helpful attitude.

## Comment #305

Wow! Harminder this is great!!!! I did not know you are an author, I love to read but more of mystery and romance. I will pass this along to the others. Maybe I will buy it for my son, he loves science. Thanks and have a wonderful day.

## Comment #306

Is there anything you don't do???? I saw your resume and it was pretty impressive already. This is really cool Harminder, Thank you for sharing.

# Comment #307

It's A lot, that's really cool. Have an awesome night Harminder!

# Comment #308

Good evening, Harminder! My name is Mikayla and I run the social media accounts at Middle Tree. I want to do a series of tutor profiles and i think you're a perfect candidate! Would you be interested? The post will include a couple of pictures of you that Linda has provided for me and a little "blurb" about yourself.

# Comment #309

Good afternoon, Thank you for your response-

# Comment #310

She said they liked meeting you but have decided to go in a different direction instead (free school tutoring). Thanks again for going out and we will call you when we have a new student in your area.

# Comment #311

You're just too cute, Harminder! Thanks so much!

# Comment #312

Thank you so much for wanting to volunteer with Promise Scholars. Attached you will find a volunteer from. If you have not filled this out already, please bring this the day of the event. Below under the "additional resources" section, I have included a link to a blog that was posted on the Huffington Post about college applications for a quick tips reference. When we arrive in the Library, where the event is to be held, we will get further instruction from the school administrators that are overseeing this event. Feel free at any time to contact me with questions.

# Comment #313

Hi Harminder! This is Stacey with Frog Tutoring! Thank you for letting me know!

# Comment #314

I'm still in need of your services as soon as possible please.

# Comment #315

Thank you again for the great tutor session. I am sending you the info for the SPSS download. Let me know if it works. Thanks again.

# Comment #316

Growing confidence in your message and gifts is a practice. It's about consistently showing up over and over again; sharing yourself; noticing what works and what doesn't; and then getting out there and doing it again. Have a beautiful month, and keep confidently shining your brilliance! You're a star, in my eyes. With love,

# Comment #317

Thank you for all the help, I appreciate it. I'll be sure to let you know if I have questions and request you for my freshen up lesson in April.- Thanks again.

# **Comment #318**

Good Job Harminder! Keep it up we always love to hear the comments from the students. You always hear the negative first but hearing the positive always makes your day better. I love it! Keep sending them. I send the feedbacks every other month so make sure to tell your students where they can add the comments re your lessons. Have an awesome day Harminder and it was nice meeting you the other day.

# **Comment #319**

So here is what I think of you: Harminder, I think you are fabulous. You are well mannered, professional, friendly, intelligent, and you want to help people. Those are some beautiful qualities in a person. I hope that one day, I will get healthier so that we can spend a little bit more time being friends.

## Comment #320

What a wonderful honor! It's nice to be thanked for your hard work and be recognized for a job well done and valued.

## Comment #321

Congratulations Harminder! Great Job.

# **Comment #322**

Hi Harmi - Thank you very much for sharing this with me. The pictures are very nice, and I am happy that they have recognized your great willingness to help others and your wonderful ability and talent in helping many people. I hope this will be a frequent occurence, since you help so many people in so many different ways. I am very proud of you. Best regards, and congratulations,

# **Comment #323**

Good for you!

# **Comment #324**

I certainly will. You are extremely intelligent and I'm grateful for the help you provided. I'm still on the mend, slowly getting better. God bless you for all you have done Harminder. And thank you again for your book. I would like to read the next one.

# **Comment #325**

Professor G. is very knowledgeable and presented many ideas on how I can better understand my statistics material. I would highly recommend him for anyone who is in need of a tutor I believe of any math subject he was very good.

## Comment #326

Thank you, Harminder, for sharing this latest update and congratulations!

## Comment #327

You do so many good things for so many people, and on top of all of that you keep taking new courses of study and learning new professions as well as daily adding to your publication list. Few people have ever been as productive and yet helpful to others. You are an inspiration to everyone that knows you.

# Comment #328

Yes, Tim saw a difference. He told me this time math's seemed easier than the previous times. When known, I'll tell you his score !Thank you for asking ! Have a nice evening!

# Comment #329

Hello. Chris is doing well at the public high school. He is taking a philosophy class beginning mid January. He's gotten his license and enjoying his independence too. Thank you for thinking of us. We hope you have a wonderful holiday as well.

## **Comment #330**

Good Morning Harminder, Thank you for checking in on Haydn. We were able to find a full time teacher for Haydn, who is working with him 6 hours a day Monday through Friday. We have enrolled him in a home studies program for credits and his instructor is developing an education in line with that. The attention and one on one instruction is helping tremendously! Thank You,

## Comment #331

Hi Harmi - I think sending her a card was very nice of you to do (and I think the correct thing to do also). Everyone needs word of comfort and praise. Best regards,

## Comment #332

We will look forward to seeing you when you have the time to come out again. I did receive your gate card. Thank you for all that you have done for the museum.

# Comment #333

Well good morning Sir.. Yes we had a great little Chat yesterday.. And it was Wonderful.. Me and My Son want to thank you for your Efforts in getting the Info to Us.. We truly appreciate it Sir and may God give you Peace Behind your Expectations in all that you Do.. Well have a Awesome and Wonderful Day.. For God has called and has Given Us another Beautiful and Amazing Day. Brother Gary.

# Comment #334

Wow! Good for you. You are very thorough and I'm sure clients appreciate that.

# comment #335

I knew you would be a super star at H & R Block but your quick progress is amazing! They are so lucky to have you. You are a smart cookie!

# Comment #336

Awe, thanks so much!!

## Comment #337

Thank You. You are so kind.

## Comment #338

Wonderful Harminder! You were one of our favorite docents at the Henry L.A. Jekel house because you weren't afraid to talk...thank you Toastmasters!

## Comment #339

Very Nice Harminder.

## Comment #340

Indeed, it was very nice talking with you today. Thank you for stopping by. I will keep your contact information for future reference.

## Comment #341

Professor, I aced my test. Thank you so much for all your help, I truly appreciate it. Very Respectfully,

## Comment #342

You should be extremely proud of yourself! Way to go Harminder! Yeah!!!

# Comment #343

To make a difference in the life of one person at a time is all the Good Lord asks of us. Good Job! When St. Theresa of Calcutta was asked she could possible make a difference with all the poor and dying, she replied, one at a time,

# Comment #344

Hello Ladies, Thank you all so very much for being a part of the makeup boot camp on Saturday. You were go kind to donate your time. I know that Harminder learned so much from all of you.

# Comment #345

Hi Niki, It was so much fun! Thank you for inviting us! I hope Harminder passed his assignment with excellence! :)

# Comment #346

Hello Harminder, I want to thank you for doing our make up. I was amazed by the before and after pictures of my make and how much better I looked with the make up. I also learned a lot from the experience and it was fun! Thanks again,

# Comment #347

Indeed, it was very nice talking with you today. Thank you for stopping by. I will keep your contact information for future reference.

# Comment #348

Thank you, I appreciate this very much and will keep you updated.

# **Comment #349**

Hello Harminder, Yes my time at Middle Tree has finished and I will be starting Pharmacy very soon this June out in Georgia. Thank you for reaching out to me, that really means a lot and I appreciate it. I enjoyed working with you and you were definitely one of the best coworkers of mine during my time at Middle Tree. Thank you again and I will definitely reach out to you if I have any questions or am in need of advice. Thank you,

## Comment #350

This is great, thank you so much!

## Comment #351

Thank you for the invitation to call 24/7. That is a very generous policy for your students. I hope they do not wake you up too often. Big Smiles,

# Comment #352

Hi! We did great. I got an A in the class and for the assignment. Thank you very much for your assistance. You helped a lot.

# Comment #353

Dear Harminder Gill, Thank you very much. Same for you, if you ever need a reference or a letter of recommendation from me saying how you helped me with my class. I also greatly appreciate your prayers for my mother and me.

# Comment #354

Hi Talia did great, she score %100. Thanks so much for your help. Can we contact you in the future if needed? Next year she is going to study geometry. Thanks again.

# Comment #355

Wonderful Harminder, Isn't it a wonderful feeling helping one person at a time be successful! Thank you for your time and patience with these students!!!

## Comment #356

Yes, I did pass the driving test, thank you.

## Comment #357

Yes, I did, and I am. Thank you for checking in!

## Comment #358

Good evening this is Aja parent. Thank you for the follow up with Aja. Yes she successful passed her driving test on the first try and has been driving safely sense.

# Comment #359

Yes, I successfully completed my driving test. I passed on my first try, and I've been successfully driving myself since April 28.

# Comment #360

Hello, thank you for checking in. I did pass my driving test, on December 26th to be exact. I am driving safely and proudly. I hope your doing good as well.

# Comment #361

Hi, I passed my test on my first try back in March. Thanks for asking.

# Comment #362

Yes, I did, thank you.

# Comment #363

Hello, Yes I did. I missed 3 I believe. thank you for your concern. I appreciate it. I will use what you taught me and drive safe.

# **Comment #364**

Hi Harminder, It was a pleasure speaking with you yesterday and I never met yet a person who finished DTM in such a short time. Looks like you are one of life time members at Toastmaster International which is great thing to know.

# **Comment #365**

Dear Harminder, You are really a smart talentedscience guy with entrepreneur minded. You wrote so many books. You like to write. Thank you for your email. Just wondering if maybe we can work together, it will be fun and we must have a lot to talk I feel. Good luck with your books and teaching!

## Comment #366

Hello, Yes, I passed my driving test and missed two points for not looking over my shoulder to look at the bike lane when turning right. Thank you for your concern.

## Comment #367

Thank you so much!

## Comment #368

Hello, sorry to get back to you so late, but I passed my test! Thanks for all the help!

# Comment #369

Good job Harminder! That must make you feel good!

# Comment #370

Excellent!

# Comment #371

Thanks a million Harminder!!

# Comment #372

Dear Harminder, Thank you! Congratulations. I hope that it went well!

# Comment #373

Dear Harminder, I am so glad you passed and got your certificate! Congratulations!

# Comment #374

Dear Harminder, Congratulations! So happy to hear you passed and received your certificate.

# Comment #375

Dear Harminder, Wonderful news. Congratulations! Big Smiles,

# Comment #376

Nice job Harminder.

# Comment #377

Good morning! Thanks so much for sharing your certificate! Great job! How did you even know you could use people from Disney for this? Great idea.

# Comment #378

Hi Harminder, Thank you for sending the review! We really appreciate it! Kind regards,

# Comment #379

Hi professor Harminder thanks again for helping me with my last driving lesson. I hope your doing well and I look forward to talking to you more. Have a good 4th of July. Sincerely,

# Comment #380

Hello Mr Gill, Thank you for taking the time to train Nadia and write this email. We appreciate you!

# Comment #381

Hey just wanted to let you know I passed

# Comment #382

Thank you very much for these notes, I appreciate it.

## Comment #383

Hello, Professor Harminder it's roby I hope you are having a nice summer so far and thanks again for helping me back June 25 for my last driving lesson. I took a vacation, went to Oregon, and came back a few days ago. Hope all is well for you take care.

## Comment #384

Hello, I passed with only 5 mistakes!

## Comment #385

Hello, she did pass with no problem at all. Thank you!

## Comment #386

Dear Prof. Gill Thanks you so much for everything. I learned so much today.

## Comment #387

Hello, I had my interview at Loma Linda and they do not require the GRE for the program I am trying to get into. If anything changes you will be my first call. Thank you for everything!

## Comment #388

Thank you for the information!

## Comment #389

Good Evening, She passed..... Thank you for asking!

## Comment #390

It went well. I passed

## Comment #391

Sounds like you're a successful driving teacher!

## Comment #392

Thanks Mr. Gill, you were an awesome teacher!

## Comment #393

Thank you Mr. Gill :) but the pictures I took of your notebook will do just fine, since it covers everything, I need to remember + outlines the driving test.

## Comment #394

Thank you! Appreciate the help

## Comment #395

Your good teaching is well appreciated by me plus your students! Thanks for doing a good job this summer.

## Comment #396

That's great! What a thoughtful man! Your diligence and integrity has been rewarded!

# **Comment #397**

Hi Harmi - I am very happy that your boss took the time and effort to thank you for your excellent work. This happens much too infrequently, and I think everyone would be happier and the world would be a better place if people would take the time to say thank you for a job well done. In any case, it is good that your boss thanked you and gave you a nice bonus. Hopefully your future bosses and colleagues will follow suit.

# Comment #398

Good morning! Wow! You must be doing an amazing job to get not only a card but cash and gift cards! Way to go!!! I'm going to share your email with Cindy!

# Comment #399

Harminder, Good for you! I am glad you were recognized for your good work. Kudos!!! Thumbs up.

## Comment #400

Professor Gill, Thank you for the letter! It meant a lot to me. I hope you are doing well. Also, thank you for investing your time in me to help me become a more mentally strong student! Respectfully

## Comment #401

God's blessings in all your endeavors!

# Comment #402

Dear Professor Gill, thank you so much for taking the time to teach my son, Jack, how to drive. Your lessons were (and will continue to be) very valuable. He passed his driving test at the Riverside East Office. Thanks again,

# Comment #403

It is always nice when people take the time to acknowledge and thank you.

## **Comment #404**

Hi Harmi - Thank you for sharing - it is indeed a very nice letter/compliment.

## **Comment #405**

Hello!! I passed! Just got my license in the mail and on the test I only missed 4 points! Thank you so much for your help!

# Comment #406

Hello, I passed my test, thank you for your help. Best,

# Comment #407

Hello Prof. Gill I passed! i only missed 7. Thank you so much for your help and notes. I appreciate it.

# Comment #408

I passed thank you!!

# **Comment #409**

Good Evening Professor Gill, This is Mehran. Thank you for sending me a letter while I was at Plebe Summer. It was great to hear from you and I appreciate you reaching out. Right now I am currently going through the academic year and I am enjoying it. It is a struggle, but it is also well worth it. Thank you for helping me get here. You spent countless hours in me and now I am finally at the Naval Academy. I can not thank you enough for that. Very Respectfully,

# Comment #410

Hello Professor Gill: Thank you for Rosalina driving lesson today below please find the correct e-mail address for Rosalina Thank You,

# Comment #411

Oh I'm just now seeing this I'm sorry, but I passed I missed 10. Thank you for checking and thank you for your services they did a great deal of help!

# Comment #412

Hi, Mr. Harminder Gill! Hana made it! Thank you for your help! Your lesson helped her so much! Sorry for not letting you know before you asked me! I'll leave a positive comment on yelp!:) If you want me to leave comments on any other website, please let me know. Thanks again!

# Comment #413

Very good. I'm proud of you. Thanks

# Comment #414

That is wonderful Harminder!

# Comment #415

Dear Harminder, Congratulations on the five star review of your successful teaching and instructing in the art and science of excellent driving performance. I am proud of you in many ways, not the least of which is your entrepreneurial outreach and results, in the field of Driver Education. I am touched and honored that you alert me to your contributions in the field of Driver Education. Allow me, belatedly, to thank you for the supportive letter you sent to me in behalf of the insensitive treatment I received on the occasion of our get together at EON following our LACE training on Saturday June 23...(it was the 23rd, was it not?) I appreciate your perspective and agree with you. It is a joy to hear from you, always. Thank you for your loving friendship and reports of your ever-enlightening experiences. You are a devoted and most appreciated friend. Warmest Regards

# **Comment #416**

Thank you, kind and 'tuned in' friend...I know I can count on you for accuracy of recall. It is a joy and a gift. Do keep me posted on your accomplishments and know that I admire your versatility and mastery of the challenges you accept and welcome. With admiration and warm regards,

## Comment #417

Wow~ You are very good Harminder. Best Wishes,

## Comment #418

He passed! Yay! Thank you for your help. With Loving Kindness,

## Comment #419

Thank you so much good night.

# Comment #420

I passed it. Thanks for all of the tips Thanks for the offer. Have a great night

# Comment #421

Hi, it's Nathan A. mom. Will he get you each time he drives? Thanks!

# Comment #422

Good morning, Harminder! What a compliment to your tutoring ability for Mehran to take the time to send you the note. He sounds very happy with the help you gave him. Great job as usual!

# Comment #423

Great to hear Harminder and Customer Service is putting that in your Tutor Profile this morning and we will log that hour for you also. Thank you for saving the day on that engagement and have a great day!

# Comment #424

Thanks Harminder. I'll let u know. Appreciate it.

# Comment #425

Passed first try Thank you very much for your help & guidance. I truly appreciate it.

# Comment #426

Yes, thank you again for your time.

# Comment #427

I passed it the first time. Thank you!

# Comment #428

This is Wisdom, I PASSED AT NORCO FIRST TRY THANK YOU FOR ALL YOUR SUPPORT AND TEACHINGS IT HELPED SO MUCH!!

# **Comment #429**

Good Morning, Harminder, Most definitely, this can be something we can look into. Thank you for this information. And Thank you once again for joining us at the meeting yesterday. I really hope it helped you in understanding a little more on how the Medicare Advantage plans work for out Medicare recipients. As previously mentioned, if you or anyone you know may have any question regarding Medicare and their approved health plans feel free to contact me. If you have any further questions or concerns feel free to contact me.

Best Regards,

# **Comment #430**

Hello Harminder, It was great meeting you at the Medicare seminar. It's always great having individuals attend to learn, and then to share that knowledge with others, thank you Harminder. Thank you for sharing about the caregiver seminar at Moreno Valley Conference Center. They have great programs there for seniors and caregivers. Also in Riverside, Parkview Community Hospital host senior and care giver seminars too. Here is their website should you like to look into what events are coming up. Hope to see you around Harminder. Take Care!

# **Comment #431**

It was also nice to meet you Gill. If you run across anyone with Medicare please send them my way. Any referrals would be greatly appreciate. Thanks for sharing your information as well. I will look into it. And thank for you for the information on the caregiver workshop. Have a wonderful rest of your week!

# Comment #432

Hey Professor Gill I just passed my driving test. Thank you for everything.

# Comment #433

Hey professed gill, i passed my driving test thanks once again.

# Comment #434

Hi Just wanted to let you know Breann passed her test. Thank you.

# Comment #435

Haydn currently has a 4.0 in school; he will be complete with his high school credits this semester and has been accepted by San Bernardino Valley College to enroll in the spring semester as a concurrent high school student. He has decided he wants to be a commercial airplane pilot so he will be enrolling in their aviation program. He has been taking flying lessons at the Riverside municipal Airport and should have his private pilot's license by the end of the year. It is hard to believe this is the same kid who was failing every class his sophomore year. He just needed a change in how he was being taught. Now he is driven, confident, and motivated. You would be very impressed.

# Comment #436

Thank you. You are so kind to remember him. He has been at Crafton for now. Enjoy your holidays as well!

# Comment #437

She ended up getting a B! She was getting a D for a while. Thanks for your help.

## Comment #438

Great Job Harminder. Congrats. Have a Happy Holiday Season! Blessings,

## Comment #439

Thank you so much You have a wonderful holiday as well.

## Comment #440

That's great Harminder. I'm sure you were a great help to Morgan. Well done.

# Comment #441

I hope you are continuing to grow and learn every day. =) You are a well mannered person. Thank you for being kind and respectful. Keep it up.

Respectfully,

# Comment #442

Great! Looks like an appreciative parent!

# Comment #443

Congratulations on your Book Launch!

## Comment #444

What a wonderful email from you Congratulations on the appealing demo web page. It is impressive in it's appearance. The dramatic way it presents your books is enticing. I also visited the web page devoted to the author: Harminder Gill. I found this page very impressive because it shared with the world your academic and professional accomplishments. So much for me to be proud of, as your friend and fan.

## Comment #445

Congratulations! That's amazing Harminder!!! Thank you for letting me know.

## Comment #446

Awesome! Thanks Harminder!

# Comment #447

He passed!! He only missed 1 point because he passed the limit line at one stop sign. But the instructor told him he did a great job Thank you so much! Happy Holidays!

# Comment #448

Good. She ended up with a B in the class. Thanks for the help! You too. I will contact you soon for more tutoring. I'm starting a new chemistry class in February. Thanks Professor Gill!

# Comment #449

Hey Professor, it's me Isaiah. Yeah I did fine my first quarter and I'm going to be taking Chemistry, Math, and English next quarter.

# Comment #450

Wow! This is huge news! Congratulations, Harminder!

# Comment #451

Hi Harminder, Suzy just told me your wonderful news! Congratulations on passing your Real Estate exam. I have heard it is a difficult test to pass! Your hard work is paying off Harminder! Great job! We are happy for your accomplishments!

# Comment #452

Wow! You're getting all kinds of skills! Good for you! Congratulations!

## Comment #453

You never cease to amaze me. That's awesome. Happy Holidays, Harminder!

## Comment #454

Hi there! My test went very well! I passed with excellence and only had 2 errors which were very minor. Thank you so much for your help! I remembered all of thegreat things you taught me while I was driving around. I also really appreciate that you remembered my test and asked how it went! I will check out your books and the website as well! I hope all goes well with the truck and motorcycle driving when you decide to take those tests! Have a good time at H&R Block! Thank you again,

## Comment #455

Excellent reinforcement for your teaching strategies!

## Comment #456

Thank you sir, I received a score of 100% on my driving test! Thank you for all of your time and training. Good luck with your new career path, I will let my parents know. Respectfully,

## Comment #457

Yes I did, it would be a year 2 months from now that I passed.

## Comment #458

Hey, Mr. Gill, Amoha got a B in her AP chemistry 1st semester.

# Comment #459

GREAT JOB!!

# Comment #460

Awesome! Thanks, Harminder! I'll pass it on!

# Comment #461

Thank you Harminder! I hope your new books get great reviews and reap tons of success. :-D

# Comment #462

Someday when they make movies from your books, I will say I knew you when.... Let's hope this happens for you. Best Wishes,

## Comment #463

Happy New Year Harminder. We miss you at the health club. thank you for continuing on contact me and letting me know how well you're doing. Best regards,

## Comment #464

Will check it out and also see if the client is still available. Thanks :)

## Comment #465

Great!!

## Comment #466

Thank you Harminder, I will let everyone know about the website. Best regards,

## Comment #467

The site looks great Harminder. Best of luck in hits and all your endeavors.

## Comment #468

Good work! Best rgs

## Comment #469

Thanks for sharing! This is really amazing! You're a hard worker Harminder. Hope you're proud of your accomplishments

## Comment #470

Congrats! I Posted it on my Facebook Page! Blessings,

# Comment #471

Thank you, Harminder! Hope you are well. Please take care.

# Comment #472

Hello Harminder, How nice to hear from you, and how very nice to see your books. That is impressive, Harminder. I am pleased to see that you are an author, and have two offerings out so far. I have not read your books, but I shall have to go on Amazon and purchase them.  What do your days look like?  How are you filling your time, and what are you attempting too accomplish currently? I would love to hear more from you.  Warmest Regards,

# Comment #473

Congrats on the new website! How are you doing? Everything good? Thank you,

# Comment #474

Mr. Gill Thank you for taking your time to deliver my package. I arrived late last night to find also this package, which is from you. Thank you so much

# Comment #475

Cool, thank you for sending! Will do

## Comment #476

Yes I already Pass my driving last year. Thanks

## Comment #477

Hello, Yes I did! I got my license on Christmas Eve.

## Comment #478

Hello again! Yes I did pass my test on 09/05/18 and I sincerely believe that it was thanks to your guidance and I am very grateful to you. Thank you!

## Comment #479

Yes I did thank you for the lesson

## Comment #480

Hey Mr. Gill Thank you for contacting me. I PASSED FIRST TRY AND THANK YOU FOR YOUR COACHING!!

## Comment #481

Good evening. I did pass my driving test back in August. Thank you for teaching me :)

# Comment #482

Oh yeah I did on the first try haha! Sorry I forgot to tell you!

# Comment #483

Passed with only 3 mistakes, one for turning on the blinker too early, one for not looking, and one for blinker too late.

# Comment #484

Hello this is Mrs. Arreglado, her mom. Yes she passed her driving test. Thanks for asking. Thanks

# Comment #485

Hello Mr. Gill,
Thank you for your follow up with Julianna.

# Comment #486

yes i did pass my driving test!

## Comment #487

Of course I remember you! Yes, I passed and only got three wrong. Thank you for teaching me for my first behind the wheel; I knew absolutely nothing at that time and you most definitely gave rise to a skill set that helped me pass. Hope you are doing well.

## Comment #488

No instructor I was afraid of not passing it. I havent attempted to take the rest again but I haven't had the oppuritunty. I can get you as instructor again?

# Comment #489

I'll definitely have a look at your books on amazon, thank you for letting me know! Any recommendations?

# Comment #490

looked for your email for so long cuz you were amazing!!!! And yea, I passed my test, thank you for all the help!! Also, I'm made it into and open class core called GOLD, and I play mellophone!

# Comment #491

yes I did pass my driving test

# Comment #492

Hello it's so nice to hear from you I really appreciate you checking in. Yes I'm glad to report I have passed and got my License in August. I failed my first try and got it my second thank god. I'm definitely grateful for your assistance and hope you're doing well!

# Comment #493

It's his mom. He passed!

# Comment #494

Hi there, This is Makenzie's mom. The other day I was telling my friend about you and how professional and courteous you were with us. Makenzie did pass her driving test. I'm glad that you found another work opportunity. Thanks for thinking about Makenzie. Take Care,

# Comment #495

Hello! I did pass my drivers test with really good scores too!

# Comment #496

Thank you for letting me know. I'll check them out!

## Comment #497

I can't think of anything. I'm quite satisfied.

## Comment #498

Excellent Harminder! You're having a positive impact! Good for you!

## Comment #499

Everything was fast and easy. My tax professional helper walked me through everything.

## Comment #500

Mr. Gill, my tax preparer, was very friendly, knowledgeable and kind.  Everyone was friendly, polite and nice to talk to.  It was an all around experience instead of just helping someone fill in some boxes.

## Comment #501

Hello,  Yes, I passed my driving test first try.  Thank you for the tips.

## Comment #502

Her daughter Sarah has done make up for the Cool Haus commercials. Your videos have helped her with new skills.

# Comment #503

Yes I did good luck at the new job.

# Comment #504

Super nice guy right always talked about upfront pricing and tried to make an appointment with me. I want to be his best friend. He seems so great.

# Comment #505

Thank you so much for you kindness, Harminder!

# Comment #506

Actually Harminder, there are many wonderful people—as I personally know them—who are encouragers, helpful, respectful, and want good things for those they meet. Continue looking for those social situations that foster and attract those types.

# Comment #507

Hoping, praying you find peace!

# Comment #508

Hello Mr. Gill, Yes, Carson passed his test and has been driving (safely) for a few months now. Thank you for checking in and good luck with your new endeavors.

# Comment #509

Fantastic efforts! We appreciate you for going out and promoting with flyers. Thank you for staying determined in striving to obtain new clients!

# Comment #510

That's awesome Harminder!! Way to go!!

# Comment #511

Congrats Harminder on reaching level 5! Go get em! Best of luck on your EA exam.

# Comment #512

Prof, Yes, Barima passed his driving test. Thanks a lot for guiding him. Greetings,

# Comment #513

Always great service. Quick easy and peace of mind. Garland's impressive he always remembers our business and personal tax needs. This year we were able to work with Harminder this year he was great too.

# Comment #514

I would kiss you because you are handsome, intelligent, kind, and interesting. You seem to dress nice too.

# Comment #515

Love it! Great pic! You're a lot cuter than I expected. Yes, I really mean it. I wasn't expecting you to be so cute.

# Comment #516

Thanks so much, Harminder! You're the best!

# Comment #517

Thank you for tutoring Lizzy at 5:45 pm tomorrow. :)

# Comment #518

Hi Harminder! Surprisingly, I received a 92% on the first exam! I was very pleased with my grade! Thank you again for all your help last week. This week has been so busy with finals for my other two classes that I have not been able to schedule a tutoring session for Physics, but hopefully I can resume tutoring next week. Hope you had fun at Disneyland!

## Comment #519

Hi there! You're always everyone's first choice! I'll let you know if I get a student today. I could have used you in Glendale this morning! Had a hard time getting a chem tutor but finally got her placed.

## Comment #520

Hi Harminder, it's Gretchen from GP Tutoring. I just called about a student Maya Piscitello, her Dad James will be contacting you to set up another skype session for Maya, she really enjoyed working with you!

# Comment #521

Hi Harminder, thanks for always coming to the rescue when we need a tutor at the last minute!

# Comment #522

I just wanted to thank you for doing an amazing job with Amber last night. I just got off the phone with her dad and he was so grateful for your help. He said that he wants to use us again once the school year starts and will ask specifically to work with you for any math/science classes. Not only for Amber, but also for his other daughter who is in college. Thanks again!!

## Comment #523

You are an amazing tutor and everyone here in the office really appreciates all that you do! Have a beautiful day :)

## Comment #524

She got an A. Thank you so much for your help!

## Comment #525

Hi Harminder!

Great job with Lizzy! Everyone thinks you're the best Skype tutor anywhere! Good morning, Harminder! I love it when you share your comments from students! You do such a great job for them and Grade Potential! I hope your summer is going well!

# Comment #526

That's awesome Harminder! You are our very best tutor in SoCal office! Thank you for always doing your best with students.

# Comment #527

Hi professor Gill. Sorry I hadn't texted back. It's Benz. Yes, both my sister and I did well in Chemistry. I passed with a B and she passed with an A. Thanks for all your help!

# Comment #528

Hi Prof. Gill! Thank you again for all your help! Her essay looks great! Morgan has gotten accepted to Alabama- 24K a year scholarship, CSU and Belmont University (Presidential Scholarship 10K a year). Thank you so much for checking in on her!

We are so thankful for all your help! I will certainty encourage Morgan to reach out if she needs any assistance. Take Care!

Hello! I remember. Morgan auditioned with a nice scholarship ($22 K each year) to Berklee College of Music. She is going to follow her passion (singing). She did get into several really good schools with scholarships but decided that Music was the way to go!

# **Letters of Recommendations**

I also wish to include past professors and supervisors who continue to be supportive. I also left the names out for confidentiality. During these changing times where the teaching profession is not the same in the past where most of the educators cared, I found it to be rare to have effective mentors to guide me and help me along the way to be the best I can continue to be. If only all professors and supervisors were like that, then we could have better instruction in our school settings which leads to better productivity and better communities. Although hard to find in society, the reader should know there are those few excellent teachers and professors out there for those who find them.

# Letter #1

To Whom It May Concern,

It is with a great pleasure that I write this letter of recommendation for Mr. Harminder Gill who is applying for a position in the Chemistry Department with the Riverside Community College District.

I have had the distinct pleasure of recruiting Mr. Gill into the Inland Empire Faculty Internship Program during the 2001-2002 academic year. Mr. Gill successfully served as one of several outstanding interns in the program. Mr. Gill took full advantage of his opportunities and served as an outstanding adjunct faculty member during the spring semester 2002. His knowledge of subject matter was well received by his mentor teachers, colleagues, and most importantly, his students during his tenure as an adjunct instructor.

To have ever made Mr. Gill's acquaintance, is to know of his personal and professional commitment to teaching. His incredible knowledge and mastery of subject matter, teaching methodologies, coupled with his congenial personality are significant attributes that are important for delivering information to students.

Mr. Gill has demonstrated an impeccable record throughout his higher educational training and preparation by all accounts of his transcript record. Throughout the internship experience, he demonstrated his ability to quickly comprehend new concepts of teaching to multicultural student populations.

Mr. Gill was mentored by one of Mt. San Jacinto College's top chemistry professors during his experience with the Inland Empire Faculty Internship Program. He has also been teaching as an adjunct instructor in the chemistry department at Riverside Community College for the past semester. I believe that the internship's unique training helped him more fully understand the expectations and demands of the community college mission, faculty, staff, and students.

Mr. Gill will be a valuable asset to any organization fortunate enough to hire him in a full-time capacity. I recommend Mr. Harminder Gill as the next Chemistry Instructor at Riverside Community College.

# Letter #2

Harminder Gill has participated in the mentorship program at Mt. San Jacinto College in the delivery of the Chemistry 100 curriculum. This is a single semester program where he has worked with a mentor developing his teaching skills.

Harminder is always well prepared for lecture. He has spent a large amount of time putting his lecture notes into Powerpoint format. This makes his lectures highly organized and easy to follow. The students are given copies of these notes enabling them to concentrate on the presented topics rather than writing and recording the information.

Harminder's lectures make use of the whiteboard, computer, and projection system. He often uses socratic questioning techniques and has students work in groups while problem solving. Students are very attentive while he is lecturing. His leture style has progressed to the point where he is giving a lot of practical examples and visual diagrams while presenting chemical concepts. This is a great aid for students trying to learn these, often difficult, concepts.

Harminder has good rapport with students. He is a compassionate person who has the best interest in the student in mind. Throughout the course of the semester he has learned to be more relaxed in front of the class. Being more relaxed has made him more approachable and has helped his rapport with students.

Harminder had communication throughout the semester. He has increased the frequency of using visual aides during lecture, often drawing diagrams on the board which help student's understand important chemical principles. He has improved his utilization of Powerpoint software as well, making his lectures more interesting and understanding. Currently, his communication skills are very good. Overall, Harminder Gill is an effective instructor.

# **Letter #3**

Members of the Search Committee

I am pleased to recommend Harminder Gill to you for the position of Instructor at your community college campus.

When I was the Coordinator of Graduate Student Programs in the Teaching Resources Center at UC Davis, Harminder successfully completed the Seminar in College Teaching in Winter 2001. This program provides graduate students with opportunities to better prepare themselves as teaching assistants while here at UC Davis. In addition, it exposes those interested in post secondary teaching careers to information and activities to develop skills important to be successful, independent instructors at the college level.

Each of the Seminar in College Teaching sessions are designed around one of nine questions that all instructors should ask themselves as they engage in instruction. *What do I want my students to learn? Who are my students? What do I do to get started? How do I best communicate the course content? How do I get students to engage and interact? Should I try something new? How do I assess student learning? What is the right thing to do? How do I get better?*

Participants completed two or more assignments which would normally be part of preparing to teach their first course; assignment choices included creating a syllabus, preparing a set of lesson parts, practicing communication skills, investigating ethical issues, and writing a teaching philosophy statement.

Current and classic readings, and exercises in teaching and learning, were available on the seminar web site to support the instruction and discussion within the sessions. Participants bridged weekly meetings by continuing discussion of session topics and weekly readings on the seminar e-mail list serve.

Harminder has kept in touch with me, and I know that he has been very focused on continuing his professional development as an instructor. He has continued to seek a range of opportunities, and has recently completed the Inland Empire Faculty Internship Program, followed by teaching as an adjunct at San Jacinto Community College, Riverside Community College, and at Mt. San

Antonio College. He knows that good instructors constantly hone their skills, and he has sought opportunities to do that; he works with students as an adult literacy tutor at theRiverside Public Library, and he actively participates in Toastmaster activities. All of these activities are indicative of a committed instructor who cares deeply about developing skills critical to support the learning of his students.

# Letter #4

Dear Harminder,

What a wonderful update on your current activities and book projects. To be a docent at the Victorian Museum is a marvelous way to share your knowledge and generate enthusiasm and appreciation for turn of the century history and life style. You are well suited to represent the grace and dignity of the period...not to mention the fun of having the hobby of continuous discovery of fresh additions to include in your presentations. Fortunate are the guests and visitors who are part of your tours. Happy to learn you continue the momentum on book projects. We miss having you with us at LACE. Thank you for your thoughtfulness in keeping us posted.

Warm regards

## **Letter #5**

We are happy that you have added to your many skills "kit", Certified Tax Preparer. Your clients are fortunate indeed to have one as patient and fastidious, as are you. We think you made the right decision to focus on the tax preparation as a priority. Thank you for the thoughtful "heads up" regarding traffic obstacles. We are pleased to have your websites. You are a "one stop does most of it all" resource. It is fun to be in your company, enjoying being with what we consider to be a "warehouse of knowledge and information."

Warm Regards

# Letter #6

Having myself worked for PBS, I had the wonderful privilege of having brilliant volunteer staff members whose creative problem solving and ingenuity was indispensable to the success of my responsibilities which involved writing and producing 450 half hour nationally syndicated television shows, distributed by WQED Television, in Pittsburgh Pennsylvania.

I mention the volunteer support I received, because I would like to recommend to you a candidate for volunteer support to you. He is a DTM Toastmaster who has taught Chemistry at Riverside University, is currently writing a book on the excitement of science. His name is Harminder Gill. I have had the pleasure of knowing him through the sharing of LACE experiences we have both attended in the past few years. Harminder so values Founders District LACE that he drives from his home District in Riverside to join us. He joins our District presenters, LACE Team and participants at "constructive hanging around time" fin a local restaurant, following the close of LACE. Last evening a large group of LACE folks, including Harminder, gather at Rutegabor restaurant on Glassell.

What impresses me is that early this morning, awaiting for me in my email "box," was an answer to my question to Harminder, "Of the LACEpresentations you attended what stands out that made your trip from Riverside to LACE at Chapman University, worthwhile.

Because the acoustics in the restaurant were not conducive to my hearing Harminder response to my question, he did what he consistently does so well: he followed through with a synopsis of what he found useful that caused him to say yesterday's LACE was well worth the effort.

I am attaching Harminder notes, because they reveal what a "steady at the wheel" gentleman he is. He is not only aware and on top of things, he is thorough, responsible, and reliable. Best of all, I have seen him evaluate, on television, a presentation at a National University made by Tristin Tucker and Erica Began. Harminder was both brilliant in his critical thinking skills and diplomatic in his comments. His voice and image project credibility and clarity.

I observed the same impressive demeanor in Cindy Carpenter's presentation, yesterday, in which she had Harminder assist with a concept she was sharing with the audience. I mentioned to Harminder that I would alert you about the possibility of a place for an enlightened volunteer to serve as a volunteer on your team. It would be a gift to have one of his strong communication skills on board as a volunteer.

I will close by saying that I will copy this email to Harminder Gill with the hope that the two of you will one day meet and perhaps arrange a volunteer spot on a project.


Warm regards,

# **Letter #7**

Dear Mr. Gill

Thank you for your time, service and assistance with the VITA Tax Preparation Assistance Workshops held at the Arlanza Library and Corona-Norco Unified School District (CNUSD) Parent Center. Our partnership fostered a great turnout and the even was a success. It was remarkable to provide these much-needed services to residents of the 60th Assembly District.

Again, I thank you for your service and look forward to continuing our working together. Should you need assistance, please do not hesitate to contact my District Office. Assembly member, 60th District.

# Letter #8

Please accept this letter as my personal recommendation for Harminder Gill. It was my pleasure to work with Harminder as a member of my team of volunteer docents at the Quality West Wing Foundation, a learning center for students. Harminder worked with our team from September 2014 to May 2015, during which time he reported to me.

Mr. Gill was an excellent member of our team. He provided a service to out learning center by working primarily with students in a computer laboratory or classroom setting. He was responsible for instructing students on how to use our computer program, assist with any questions in the classroom and troubleshoot when a student had difficulties with their assigned tasks. He successfully completed his duties and enabled our students/visitors navigate through our curriculum.

Mr. Gill displayed a tremendous amount of dedication and trustworthiness. He contributed to our educational program and worked many hours to help achieve our goals. He also developed a wonderful rapport with other members of our volunteer team and displayed a strong character and moral fiber. I admire Mr. Gill's determination and enjoyed working with him. He was an asset to our educational program and I would not hesitate to work with him again. I wish him well in his future endeavors and have the utmost of confidence in him.

Please contact me should you require further information.


Education Director


Quality West Wing Foundation

# Letter #9

It is an honor writing this letter of recommendation for Harminder for consideration for Care. comAs his supervisor I have witnessed Harminder commitment to customer service. Harminder has donated over One Hundred Forty-Five (145) hours of volunteer service in the Riverside Medical Center's Department of Education. He began his volunteer service on 07/27/2009. We have kept in touch via e-mail. In his duties, I found that no job was beneath Harminder, as he actively sought out learning opportunities and offered support whenever needed. His individual abilities combined with his quest for participation and overall inquisitiveness for life puts Harminder in a unique group of individuals. As a volunteer, Harminder continually demonstrated a mature sense of ethical righteousness, compassion for his fellow man, and commitment to high ideals. Riverside Medical Center's Department of Education appreciates Harminder assistance, flexibility, and commitment to maintaining workflow. Harminder is a team player and will roll up his sleeves and go beyond the call of duty when asked by his coworkers. His patience and attitude make me believe he would be a compassionate, knowledgeable, and talented professor. As you can see, Harminder has proven to be an energetic individual; one whose success equals his sincerity and work ethic. It is with pleasure that I recommend Harminder. I know that if given the opportunity Harminder will prove himself by working hard. Thank you for your time and consideration. If you have, any questions please feel free to contact me.

# Letter #10

This letter is to very highly recommend Mr. Harminder Gill for your teaching position. I have known Harminder for the past twenty-seven years. During the first part of this period, he was a student in my Math. Nine ABC classes (First Year Calculus), and over the years we have had many wideranging conversations since then, so I think I know him quite well.

Harminder was an excellent student. He finished among the top five students (out of about 300 students) in all three of my classes and he got three A+'s from me. He was always in class on time, his homework was always done neatly, completely, on time, and usually perfectly, and he wrote excellent test papers. He was really interested in learning course material, rather than just memorizing to get a good grade. He is very intelligent, he took a real interest in his courses, and he was willing to work long and hard to master all aspects of them, and this combination made him a first rate student. His performance in my three classes was good enough that I rank him in the upper 3-5 percent of all undergraduates I have known (on average over 200 students each quarter).

In addition, Harminder is an excellent researcher - he is inventive. he very carefully plans ahead, he is alert to monitor and make necessary changes, and he sticks with it to the end.

Further, Harminder students (in the lab classes he TA'd) liked having him for their teacher. He does a nice job of answering his students' questions and of helping them understand the concepts involved. He carefully prepares his lesson plans, he always includes helpful and interesting applications, and he tries to help his students understand why things work, as well as how they work. He encourages class participation and always makes his students feel free to ask questions. He is generous with his office hours, and he puts considerable effort into helping his students learn.

Finally, Harminder is a very nice young man. He has a quiet, but friendly, personality and he gets along well with most people. He is courteous, cooperative, conscientious, trustworthy, and reliable, and he is always neat and well groomed. He has many other fine qualities that should help him excel in the future, and everything I know about him is positive. He has set high standards and goals for his life, he is currently living up to these standards, and he has the ability and potential to achieve his goals.

Thus, in summary, I consider Harminder to be an excellent student and young researcher, a very good teacher, and a young man of very high quality. I therefore very highly recommend him to you.

We seem to be drawn teachers and to professors who are effective to all of us. We recognize something about them that makes them special, and in fact, those qualities resonate with us for many years after leaving that professor's classroom setting. We cherish many portraits of those effective teachers and professors. Effective teaching is a combination of many factors which includes the teacher's or professor's background and the ways interacting with others as well as specific teaching and research practices.

The effective educator recognizes complexity, communicates clearly, and serves conscientiously. To succeed in the teaching profession, you must have sufficient knowledge of content, a pedagogy of context, and students to appreciate the intricacies found in the teaching and learning processes. An understanding of the complexity prevents the educator from trivializing content and underestimating the work it takes to prepare lessons. Understanding the complexity of the subject matter is reflected in an effort it takes to implement lessons with students.

Effective educators recognize each student as unique individuals by understanding each one brings her own set of experiences and perspectives to the classroom setting. Effective educators recognize a class is a dynamic and multifaceted entity, which is made up of a myriad of personalities one must deal with. These understandings contribute to a educator's interactions with students, practices for managing the environment, and preparation and differentiation for student learning needs. Effective educators understand and can successfully navigate through complexity. They simultaneously handle multiple tasks and multiple meanings without losing sight of the goal for moving toward their specific destination.

Communication is crucial for the success in any profession that requires interaction among people and within an organization. The teaching job requires clear articulation of expectations, encouragement, caring, and updated content knowledge. Communicating content in teaching is far more than talking about the objectives. Having effective communication requires the educator to have a clear understanding of the subject matter and how to share the material with students that they come to own and understand it deeply.

Effective educators teach content knowledge, skills, and be adept at facilitating students search for knowledge. Remember an educator must continue to communicate a climate of support and encouragement to ensure students are engaged in a two-way teaching and learning process. Effective management and student learning are related to communications of expectations. Being an effective communicator is about delivering the message so that someone can receive, respond, and use the information successfully.

Effective educators need to be willing to dedicate both time and energy to the profession. It is better to work both hard and smart. They are concerned with their own continuous learning process and reflect on all elements of performance in their efforts to continually improve.

Effective educators care about students, and ensures the students can recognize the caring and feeling of being supported and encouraged. They care about the classroom setting and strives to make sure there is an organized and positive learning environment. Conscientious reflection and the involvement in the aspects of teaching is critical in defining effective educators.

Many characteristics of effective educators can be found in by just awareness brought by observing other excellent teachers or professors, receiving peer feedback, cultivating collegial relationships, and getting involved with lifelong learning experiences. High-quality professional development activities are necessary for improving effectiveness in the teaching profession.

The activities need to be collegial, challenging, and a socially positive atmosphere since learning entails these kinds of characteristics. Professional development training should be tailored to individual teachers or professors within the particular school to support both the individual and organizational needs. Teaching should always be a ongoing and deliberate process that never ends.

By examining the prerequisites of effective teaching, looking at the teacher or professor as a person, dealing with classroom management, and carrying out the teaching and learning process are qualities effective professors should follow.

Teaching effectiveness draws on multitude of skills and attributes from different combinations and in different contexts that give results that define effectiveness.

Effective teachers or professors whose teaching is marked by many teaching strategies has had solid educational preparation through coursework and professional development. The educator can employ good instructional strategies because the classroom is well managed which provides time to employ the strategies. Having good rapport with students is based on maintaining appropriate roles. This requires clarity in behavioral expectations and consistency when dealing with disciplinary situations.

Furthermore, three important points when it comes to effective teaching, which includes knowledge, and caring as being important attributes communication and classroom management, and the process and mastery being important products of teaching. The educator's background and the educator's teaching processes are important, but are still not enough to carry out effective teaching. The best proof of teaching effectiveness is achieving student results. This involves more time spent in the classroom setting. Students should be able to read better, carry out math problems, having a better understanding of their place in the world, and show worthy achievements. Measuring professor's success by teaching processes is not enough. Positive outcomes are the ones that count.

Remember the educator is the representative of the subject curriculum in the school setting. How a educator presents oneself makes an impression on administrators, colleagues, parents, students, and community members. A educator who shows enthusiasm and competence for the subject area transfer those feelings to the students.

How the educator relates to students has an impact on the students experiences in the classroom setting. The professor's personality is probably the first set of characteristics to look for in an effective professor. It is doable to help improve one's teaching, but it is difficult to change one's personality.

Positive qualities to look for in an effective educator include assuming ownership in the classroom and achieving student success, using personal experiences as examples in the teaching profession, understanding the feelings of students, being able to communicate in a clear and concise fashion, admitting mistakes and being able to correct them, reflects about their practice on teaching, has a sense of humor, dresses appropriately for the teaching position, and maintains confidential trust and respect which is not hard to do at this day and age.

Other positive qualities to look for include being structured and flexible, being able to respond to situations and the needs for students, enjoys teaching and having students also enjoy the learning process, establish win-win solutions when conflict arises, being a good listener, responds to students with respect during difficult times, and communicates high expectations on a consistent basis.

It is also important to conduct one-on-one conversations with students, treat them fairly, have positive conversations with students outside the classroom setting, spend time with single students or a small group of students outside the classroom setting, addresses students by their names, works actively with students, speaks in an appropriate tone of voice, and maintain a professionalmanner at all times.

Let us take a look at some red flags I've found in the teaching profession. I've found ineffective educators think that teaching is just another dull job, constantly arriving late to class, could care less of discipline problems, not sensitive to a student's culture, expresses bias, works on their own paperwork during class time instead of helping students, parents complaining what is going on in the classroom setting, and even uses inappropriate language in a school setting. It is also not a good idea to ridicule other students, show defensive behavior, get confrontational with students, does not care about conflict resolution skills, and does not accept responsibility to what is taking place in the classroom.

We talked about classroom management and organization in the earlier chapters. Positive qualities include positioning chairs in groups to promote interaction, manage classroom procedures to facilitate instruction, manage student behavior through clear expectations, maintain a proper physical environment, have students welcome visitors and speakers to the classroom setting, addressing students in a positive and respectful manner, and encourage interactions about activities.

Other positive qualities in the classroom setting include maximizing the physical aspects of the environment, takes care of emergency situations, maintains personal workspace, establishes rules and procedures, provides positive reinforcement, disciplines students with respect, shows consistency in management style, and post appropriate safety procedures.

There are red flags to look for in classroom settings such as carrying out inconsistencies in enforcing class and There are red flags to look for in classroom settings such as carrying out inconsistencies in enforcing class and school rules, not prepared for common issues, rank students progress for everyone to see, does not follow expectations of the students, does not display classroom rules, allow students disengaged from the learning process, not available for students outside of class, and complains inappropriately about how the administration should be carried out.

Other red flags to look for in classroom settings include maintaining an unsafe environment, have no specific routines or responsibilities, keeps the place unclean and disorderly, uses way too many disciplinary referrals, makes up consequences based on the educator's mood, and does not start class immediately. These are some negative signs to look for in a classroom setting.

Positive qualities for organizing instruction include having lesson plans written for every school day, daily plans are used based on an agenda, student assessment and diagnostic data should be available, having assessment data and pretest results available, work samples from students are available and considered when writing lesson plans, lesson plans aligned with division curriculum guides, teacher-developed assessments, learning objectives incorporated into the lesson plans, materials available when it is needed, lesson plans include strategies available for different levels, lesson plans addressing different types of learning styles, state standards being posted, pacing information, and lesson plans for substitute professors who care to teach.

Some red signs to look for when organizing and orienting instruction include few lesson plans being available, student assessment and diagnostic data not being available, no connection between assessment data and lesson plans, no different types of instruction, lesson plans not being aligned with curriculum guides, learning objectives not being incorporated into lesson plans, activities unrelated to the learning objectives, not having plans for anticipating problems, lesson plans consisting of only worksheets, and students not engaged in learning.

Other red signs to look for include lesson plans that do not address different learning styles for different students, lesson plans being disjointed, lesson plans being short and don't allow for smooth transitions between activities, inconsistent student achievement, emergency lesson plans not available, and materials for substitutes not available.

Positive qualities for implementing instruction include using student questions to guide lesson plans, using pre-assessments to guide instructions, develops elements for effective lessons, uses established routines to have more time for classroom settings, incorporates higher-order thinking strategies, uses variety of strategies to engage with students, and continuously monitor student engagement for all activities.

Other positive qualities for implementing instruction include having high numbers of student in engage in the class, adjust the delivery of the lesson plan based on student cues, use all space of the classroom and lecture hall, having a student-centered classroom, designs assignments based on objectives, assist students planning homework assignments, and provide feedback.

Red signs for ineffective teaching include constantly experiencing student behavior problems, students being unengaged, poor student performance in the class, vague instructions, not responding to student cues, lacks variety of instructional methods, has difficulty taking time for individual instruction, uses outdated material, fails to implement changes recommended by peers or supervisors, simple tell students to know the material, does not apply current strategies, use poor examples, and transitions slowly between activities.

Positive qualities for monitoring progress include enabling students to track their own progress, taking time to grade homework, give oral and written feedback, document student progress and assign positive achievement, make proper instructional decisions, circulates in the room, assigns pretests, graph results, gives multiple assessments to determine whether a student has mastered the skill, and keeps a log of parent communication.

Other positive qualities to look for when monitoring student progress include using student intervention plans, carry out team conferences, constantly give assessments, use a variety of assessments, carry out differentiated instruction based on assessment analysis, maintain copies of all correspondence, communicates about informal progress reports, and uses appropriate and clear language when communicating.

Red signs to look for include not taking the time to monitor student progress or allow for students to ask questions, lacking appropriate data, fails to monitor student progress, does not keep a communication log, does not attend conferences, gives out inflated grading such as high failure rates or high excellent grades, fail to teach again after assessments in order to correct gaps in student learning, offers no assessments, ignores special testing needs, use vague or inappropriate language in communications, and has a I don't care attitude.

Finally, let us take a look at positive professional qualities for effective educators. Positive qualities include practicing being honest as a two-way communication between all parties, communicates with families of students, takes the time to maintain accurate records, reflects on teaching, a team player, attends faculty committee meetings, focuses on students, always perform assigned duties, implement goals and policies, volunteers to help others, and takes the time to seek community involvement.

Other positive qualities include seeking leadership roles in school settings, contacts office personnel when needed, treats colleagues with respect, works collaboratively and fairly with both faculty and staff, attends professional development opportunities, maintains current in the fields of teaching, writes grammatically correct sentences, writes appropriately for the intended audience, submits grades on time, keep a record of accurate grades, and maintain a report of deadlines.

Red signs to look for include giving negative feedback, showing an unwillingness to contribute to the teaching profession, refuses to meet with parents of caring and trusting individuals, threatened by other adults who visit the classroom, carries out the minimum to maintain certification, submits reports late all the time, submits grades late all the time, writes inaccurate reports, and doesn't update their gradebook. I've only mention a few red signs for each category. There are many more, but I would like to focus more on the positive as this is the focus of the book.

A great educator is one a student remembers and cherishes forever. Great teachers or professors inspire students towards greatness. Remember all the great points I talked about including having an engaging personality and different teaching styles, clear objectives for the lessons, effective discipline skills, strong classroom management skills, consistent communication with the parents, having high expectations, knowledge of the subject matter, knowledge of curriculum and standards, passion for teaching, patience, intellectual curiosity, confidence, mentorship, enthusiasm, strong rapport with students, and a vision.

When you look back at all of your teachers or professors, think about that teacher or professor who was able to meet your learning needs within the classroom setting. Consider how the teacher or professor communicated that made the concepts and learning material to make sense. Imagine what did it take to make that favorite teacher or professor create a positive experience in which you took the time to study and learn the material. This is what I call being an effective professor who has mastery of excellent teaching. If I can't persuade you to practice your teaching, then I can't help you to improve to your ability to teach. Only you can make the decision for yourself to be that exceptional educator.

Congratulations for making it this far in the book. If you made it this far, then you are likely wanting to improve and get better at teaching. What you do at this point will determine whether you reach exceptional levels of excellence.

Improving your ability to teach can improve your ability to present and persuade affects your everyday life. Never accept average but always continue learning new ideas year after year. Every conversation and contact you have with your students can turn out to be a learning experience with them both in and out of the classroom setting. This is not the end to mastery of excellence teaching, but a window to a higher level of techniques that never ends and leads to success!

The future workforce requires students to think at higher levels and be innovative designing new products. The educational system should incorporate how students learn and effective methods to teach students. Operate your classrooms professionally, efficiently, and above all successfully.

The great teacher or professor who is the boss provides learning opportunities, new experiences, seminars, reading lists, and on the job trainings as well as hands on activities. They become great bosses by knowing that the best people are the learners, and learners gravitate towards the educator. Educators learn what they teach. Excellent educators who become great bosses teach, and attract the best people on their team. To all educators out there who care about the teaching profession, I express my sincere best wishes - May your days in teaching be filled with successful students!

# **Inspirational Quotes**

"A good teacher affects eternity; he can never tell where his influence stops." Henry Adams

"Those who know do. Those who understand, teach. We are what we repeatedly do. Excellence, then, is not an act, but a habit." Aristotle

"The greatest accomplishment is not in never falling, but in rising again after you fall." Confucius

"Logic will get you from A to B. Imagination will take you everywhere." Albert Einstein


"The secret in education lies in respecting the student." Ralph Waldo Emerson


"Tell me and I forget. Teach me and I remember. Involve me and I learn." Benjamin Franklin


"Live as if you were to die tomorrow. Learn as if you were to live forever." Mahatma Gandhi


"Better than a thousand days of diligent study is one day with a great teacher." Japanese Proverb

"The beautiful thing about learning is that no one can take it away from you."
B.B. King


"Education is the most powerful weapon which you can use to change the world."
Nelson Mandela


"What we learn with pleasure we never forget" Alfred Mercier


"Education is what survives when what has been learned has been forgotten."
B.F. Skinner


"The more that you read, the more things you will know, the more that you learn, the more places you'll go." Dr. Seuss

"I can do what you can't do, and you can do what I can't do; together we can do great things." Mother Teresa

"The mediocre teacher tells. The good teacher explains. The superior teacher demonstrates. The great teacher inspires."William A. Ward

"Education is not the filling of a pail, but the lighting of a fire." William Butler Yeats

# **References**

Parkay, Forest W. Becoming a Teacher Fifth Edition. Massachusetts: A Pearson Education Company., 2001. Print. 1-578.

Stronge James H. Qualities of Effective Teachers. Virginia: Association for Supervision and Curriculum Development, 1992. Print. vii-117.

Purdy, Scott. Time Management for Teachers Essential Tips and Techniques Second Edition. California: Write Time Publishing, 1999. Print. 1-147.

Teele, Sue. Rainbows of Intelligence Exploring How Students Learn. California: Sue Teele and Associates, 1999. Print. 1-153.

Olney, Claude W. Where There's a Will There's an A, How to Get Better Grades in College, 1999.

Koegl, Timothy J. The Exceptional Presenter. A Proven Formula to Open Up! and Own the Room. Texas: Greenleaf Book Group Press, 2007. Print. 1-186.

Amblee, R.S. The Art of Looking Into The Future The Five Principles of Technological Evolution. Connecticut: Libraries Unlimited/Teacher Ideas Press, 2011. Print. 1-367.

Maxwell, John C. The Maxwell Daily Reader. Tennessee: Thomas Nelson Inc., 2007. Print. 1-405.

Maxwell, John C. Equipping 101 What Every Leader Needs to Know. Tennessee: Thomas Nelson Inc., 2003. Print. 1-95.

Maxwell, John C. Self-Improvement 101 What Every Leader Needs to Know. Tennessee: Thomas Nelson Inc., 2009. Print. 1-107.

Maxwell, John C. The 360o Leader Developing Your Influence from Anywhere in the Organization. Tennessee: Thomas Nelson, Inc., 2011. Print. 1-356.

Maxwell, John C. Developing The Leader Within You. Developing The Leaders Around You. Tennessee: Thomas Nelson Inc., 1993 and 1995. Print. 1-413.

Robertson, Jeanne. Humor The Magic of Genie Seven Potions for Developing a Sense of Humor. Texas: Rich Publishing Co.,1990. Print. 9-216.

Carnegie, Dale. How to Develop Self-Confidence & Influence People by Public Speaking. New York: Pocket Books A Division of Simon & Schuster Inc., 2011. Print 1-198.

Calabrese, Raymond; Allain Susan; Binovi, Jeanne; Guadiano, Theresa; Ruff, William; Trautwein, Blare. A Companion Guide to Leadership for Safe Schools. Lanham, Maryland, London: Scarecrow Press, Inc., 2002. Print. 1-105.


Jensen, Eric. Student Success Secrets Fifth Edition. New York: Barron's Educational Series Inc., 2003. Print. 1-242.


Best Careers for Teachers Making the Most of Your Teaching Degree. New York: Learning Express, LLC, 2010. Print. 1-175.


Fry, Ron. How to Study Sixth Edition. New York: Delmar Cengage Learning, 2010. Print. 1-241.


Daresh, John C.; Lynch, Jane. Improve Learning by Building Community A Principal's Guide to Action. California: A Corwin Sage Company, 2010. Print. 1-135.

Power, Brenda Miller. Taking Note Improving Your Observational Notetaking. York, Maine: Stenhouse Publishers, 1996. Print. 1-96.

Armstrong, W.H.; Larpe, M.W.; Ehrenhaft, G. A Pocket Guide to Correct Study Tips Fourth Edition. New York: Barron's Education Series, Inc., 1997. Print. 1-297.

Culp, Barbara D. Essential Knowledge for Teachers Truths to Energize, Engage Today's Teachers. Maryland: Rowman & Little Field, 2017. Print. 1-73.

**The New Book of Popular Science Technology 6.**
Scholastic Library Publishing, Inc., 2008. Print. 1-446.

Fox, Jeffrey J. How To Become A Great Boss The Rules for Getting and Keeping the Best Employees. New York: Hyperion Special Markets, 2002. Print. 1-167.

Harvard Business Review Press. Emotional Intelligence Dealing with Difficult People. Massachusetts: Harvard Business School Publishing, 2018. Print. 1-136.

Masson-Draffen, Carrie. 151 Quick Ideas to Deal with Difficult People. New Jersey: The Career Press, Inc., 2007. Print. 1-181.

Howard, Linda Gordon. The Sexual Harassment Handbook. New Jersey: The Career Press, Inc., 2007. Print. 1-212.

Tiki-Toki. A History of Education Timeline. https://www.tiki-toki.com/timeline/entry/56733/A-History-of-Education-Timeline/#vars!date=2000-11-18_16:50:27!

Smith System. Education Trend. https://smithsystem.com/smithfiles/2017/03/16/futuristic-classrooms-make-way-big-changes/

Cummins, Eleanor. These Are the World's 14 Most Futuristic Schools. From boat schools to surveillance classrooms, this is the future of education. Architecture, Design & Engineering. August 4, 2017. https://www.inverse.com/article/35086-most-futuristic-schools

Day, Erick. 5 New Teaching Methods Improving Education. Getting Smart. October 6, 2017. https://www.gettingsmart.com/2017/10/5-new-teaching methods-improving-education/

Poh, Michael. 8 Technologies That Will Shape Future Classrooms. Hongkiat. July 8, 2017. https://www.hongkiat.com/blog/future-classroom technologies/

Ramey, Karehka. Future of Technology in Education. Techucation. November 7, 2012. https://www.useoftechnology.com/future-technology education/

Grantham, Nick. Five Future Technologies That Will Shape Our Classroom. George Lucas Educational Foundation. Eductopia. April 10, 2012. https://www.edutopia.org/blog/five-future-education-technologies-nick-grantham

Catone, Josh. What is the Future of Teaching. Mashable. Entertainment. August 31, 2009. https://mashable.com/2009/08/31/online-education teachers/

Donor's Choose. The 50 Most Inspirational Quotes for Teachers. March 6, 2015. https://www.curatedquotes.com/quotes-for-teachers/

# About the Author

Harminder Gill did his undergraduate studies at the University of California, Riverside, where he finished his Bachelor of Science degree in biological chemistry with an emphasis on chemistry. After completing his undergraduate studies, he attended graduate school at the University of California, Davis, where he finished his master's degree in organic chemistry. After doing several teaching assignments, he went into the teaching profession at community colleges. He was an adjunct professor at many community colleges in Southern California. He became a life member for both the alumni associations at UCR and UCD. He has done homeschooling throughout communities, where he offers more than two hundred sections of academic subjects from humanities, social sciences, sciences, and test preparation. Plenty of his past students have done exceptionally well, including those who have achieved high scores on standardized tests, getting accepted into training academies, universities, and programs of their choice. He has served on board of directors completed the distinguished toastmaster (DTM) in the Toastmasters Program for Public Speaking and Leadership, a past docent at many museums and a science institute, and now has become a tax professional and received his licenses in life insurance and real estate.

Publishing by: **Maple Leaf Publishing Inc.**
3rd Floor 4915 54 Street
Red Deer, Alberta T4N 2G7, Canada

https://mapleleafpublishinginc.com

To order additional copies of this book, contact:
**1-(403)-356-0255**

N° ISBN : **978-1-77419-014-2**

Rev. date : **12/02/2019**

Cover creation : **Marissa Flordelis**

Layout : **Marissa Flordelis**